**FOURTH EDITION**

# Java Pocket Guide

*Robert Liguori and Patricia Liguori*

Beijing · Boston · Farnham · Sebastopol · Tokyo    O'REILLY®

# Java Pocket Guide

by Robert Liguori and Patricia Liguori

Published by O'Reilly Media, Inc., 1005 Gravenstein Highway North, Sebastopol, CA 95472.

O'Reilly books may be purchased for educational, business, or sales promotional use. Online editions are also available for most titles (*http://oreilly.com/safari*). For more information, contact our corporate/institutional sales department: 800-998-9938 or *corporate@oreilly.com*.

**Editor:** Brian Foster
**Production Editor:** Justin Billing
**Copyeditor:** Amanda Kersey
**Proofreader:** Marta Justak
**Indexer:** Ellen Troutman-Zaig
**Interior Designer:** David Futato
**Cover Designer:** Karen Montgomery
**Illustrator:** Rebecca Demarest

September 2017:        Fourth Edition

**Revision History for the Fourth Edition**
> 2017-08-25:   First Release
> 2017-11-10:   Second Release

See   *http://oreilly.com/catalog/errata.csp?isbn=9781491938690*   for   release details.

978-1-491-93869-0

[LSI]

*This book is dedicated to our beautiful daughter, Ashleigh.*

# Table of Contents

# Preface

Designed to be your companion, this *Pocket Guide* provides a quick reference to the standard features of the Java programming language and its platform.

This *Pocket Guide* provides you with the information you will need while developing or debugging your Java programs, including helpful programming examples, tables, figures, and lists.

Java coverage in this book is representative through Java SE 9 incorporating a subset of the 80+ JDK Enhancement Proposals (JEPs) slated for the release. This Java coverage includes improvements to the generage language as well as coverage of the new Java Shell and the new Java Module System. This book supercedes the three previous versions: *Java Pocket Guide*, *Java 7 Pocket Guide*, and *Java 8 Pocket Guide*.

For uniformity and enhanced interest, the majority of the code examples in this fourth edition of the *Java Pocket Guide* have been updated from code segments of the Gliesians Web Application. At the time of this writing, the primary focus of the Gliesians Web Application is to provide free utilities relative to genealogy and small unmanned aerial systems.

The material in this book also provides support in preparing for the Oracle Certified Programmer exams. If you are considering pursuing one of the Java certifications, you may also wish to acquire the *OCA Java SE 8 Programmer I Study Guide (Exam 1Z0-808)* by Edward Finegan and Robert Liguori (McGraw-Hill Osborne Media, 2015).

# Book Structure

This book is broken into three parts: Part I details the Java programming language as derived from the Java Language Specification (JLS) and JEPs. Part II details Java platform components and related topics. Part III is the appendixes covering supporting technologies.

# Conventions Used in This Book

The following typographical conventions are used in this book:

*Italic*

> Indicates new terms, URLs, email addresses, filenames, and file extensions.

`Constant width`

> Used for program listings, as well as within paragraphs to refer to program elements such as variable or function names, databases, data types, environment variables, statements, and keywords.

**`Constant width bold`**

> Shows commands or other text that should be typed literally by the user.

*`Constant width italic`*

> Shows text that should be replaced with user-supplied values or by values determined by context.

---

**TIP**

This element signifies a tip, suggestion, or general note.

---

---

**WARNING**

This element indicates a warning or caution.

---

# O'Reilly Safari

---

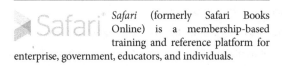 *Safari* (formerly Safari Books Online) is a membership-based training and reference platform for enterprise, government, educators, and individuals.

---

Members have access to thousands of books, training videos, Learning Paths, interactive tutorials, and curated playlists from over 250 publishers, including O'Reilly Media, Harvard Business Review, Prentice Hall Professional, Addison-Wesley Professional, Microsoft Press, Sams, Que, Peachpit Press, Adobe, Focal Press, Cisco Press, John Wiley & Sons, Syngress, Morgan Kaufmann, IBM Redbooks, Packt, Adobe Press, FT Press, Apress, Manning, New Riders, McGraw-Hill, Jones & Bartlett, and Course Technology, among others.

For more information, please visit *http://oreilly.com/safari*.

# How to Contact Us

Please address comments and questions concerning this book to the publisher:

    O'Reilly Media, Inc.
    1005 Gravenstein Highway North
    Sebastopol, CA 95472
    800-998-9938 (in the United States or Canada)
    707-829-0515 (international or local)
    707-829-0104 (fax)

We have a web page for this book, where we list errata, examples, and any additional information. You can access this page at *http://bit.ly/java-pocket-guide-4e*.

To comment or ask technical questions about this book, send email to *bookquestions@oreilly.com*.

For more information about our books, courses, conferences, and news, see our website at *http://www.oreilly.com*.

Find us on Facebook: *http://facebook.com/oreilly*

Follow us on Twitter: *http://twitter.com/oreillymedia*

Watch us on YouTube: *http://www.youtube.com/oreillymedia*

## Acknowledgments

We extend a special thank you to all the folks at O'Reilly. Appreciation of support also goes out to Greg Grockenberger and Ryan Cuprak, who wrote for the JShell and Java Module System chapters, respectively. Ryan also performed the technical review of the book, which we appreciate.

We would also like to thank again all of those who participated with the original *Java Pocket Guide*, the *Java 7 Pocket Guide*, and the *Java 8 Pocket Guide*.

Additional appreciation to people not related to this book project: Don Anderson, David Chong, Keith Cianfrani, Jay Clark, Steve Cullen, Ed DiCampli, Phil Greco, Scott Houck, Cliff Johnson, Juan Keller, Fran Kelly, Mike Krauss, Mike Lazlo, Phil Maloney, Lana Manovych, Matt Mariani, Chris Martino, Roe Morande, Sohrob Mottaghi, Brendan Nugent, Keith Smaniotto, Tom Tessitore, Lacey Thompson, Tyler Travis, Justin Trulear, and Jack Wombough.

We would finally like to thank all of our family members for always being there for us.

# PART I
# Language

# CHAPTER 1

# Naming Conventions

Naming conventions are used to make Java programs more readable. It is important to use meaningful and unambiguous names comprised of Java letters. The following examples are from various Java sources.

## Acronyms

When using acronyms in names, only the first letter of the acronym should be uppercase and only when uppercase is appropriate:

```java
// e.g., DNA is represented as Dna
public class GliesianDnaProvider {...}

// e.g., Most Recent Common Ancestor (MRCA) is Mrca
public class MrcaCalculator {...}
```

## Annotation Names

Annotation names have been presented several ways in the Java SE API for predefined annotation types, [*adjective*|*verb*] [*noun*]:

```java
@Documented
@Retention(RetentionPolicy.RUNTIME)
```

```
@Target(ElementType.TYPE)
public @interface FunctionalInterface {}
```

# Class Names

Class names should be nouns, as they represent "things" or "objects." They should be mixed case (camel case) with only the first letter of each word capitalized, as in the following:

```
public class AirDensityCalculator {...}
```

# Constant Names

Constant names should be all uppercase letters, and multiple words should be separated by underscores:

```
private static final double KELVIN = 273.16;
private static final double DRY_AIR_GAS_CONSTANT =
287.058;
private static final double HUMID_AIR_GAS_CONSTANT
= 461.4964;
```

# Enumeration Names

Enumeration names should follow the conventions of class names. The enumeration set of objects (choices) should be all uppercase letters:

```
public enum MeasurementSystem {
  METRIC, UNITED_STATES_CUSTOMARY, IMPERIAL
}

public enum Study {
  ALL, NON_ENDOGAMOUS, SEMI_ENDOGAMOUS, ENDOGAMOUS
}

public enum RelationshipMatchCategory {
  IMMEDIATE, CLOSE, DISTANT, SPECULATIVE
}
```

# Generic Type Parameter Names

Generic type parameter names should be uppercase single letters. The letter T for type is typically recommended.

The Collections Framework makes extensive use of generics. E is used for collection elements, S is used for service loaders, and K and V are used for map keys and values:

```
public interface Map <K,V> {
    V put(K key, V value);
}
```

# Instance and Static Variable Names

Instance and static variable names should be nouns and should follow the same capitalization convention as method names:

```
private String prediction;
```

# Interface Names

Interface names should be adjectives. They should end with "able" or "ible" whenever the interface provides a capability; otherwise, they should be nouns. Interface names follow the same capitalization convention as class names:

```
public interface Relatable {...}
public interface SystemPanel {...}
```

# Method Names

Method names should contain a verb, as they are used to make an object take action. They should be mixed case, beginning with a lowercase letter, and the first letter of each subsequent word should be capitalized. Adjectives and nouns may be included in method names:

```
public void clear() {...} // verb
public void toString() // preposition and noun
public double getDryAirDensity() {...} // verb,
```

```
adjective and noun
public double getHumidAirDensity() {...} // verb,
adjective and noun
```

# Package Names

Package names should be unique and consist of lowercase letters. Underscores may be used if necessary:

```
// Gliesian.com (company), JAirDensity (software)
package com.gliesian.jairdensity;

// Gliesian.com (company), FOREX Calculator (soft
ware), Utilties
package com.gliesian.forex_calculator.utils;
```

Publicly available packages should be the reversed internet domain name of the organization, beginning with a single-word top-level domain name (e.g., *com, net, org,* or *edu*), followed by the name of the organization and the project or division. (Internal packages are typically named according to the project.)

Package names that begin with java and javax are restricted and can be used only to provide conforming implementations to the Java class libraries.

# Module Names

Module names should be the reversed internet domain name with the same guidelines as package names:

```
module com.gliesian.utils {
}
```

# Parameter and Local Variable Names

Parameter and local variable names should be descriptive lowercase single words, acronyms, or abbreviations. If multiple words are necessary, they should follow the same capitalization convention as method names:

---

```
public void printPredictions (ArrayList predic
tions) {
  int counter = 1;
  for (String prediction : predictions) {
    System.out.println("Predictions #" + counter++
+ ": " + prediction);
  }
}
```

Temporary variable names may be single letters such as i, j, k, m, and n for integers and c, d, and e for characters. Temporary and looping variables may be one-character names as shown in Table 1-1.

*Table 1-1. Temporary and looping variables*

| One-character name | Type |
| --- | --- |
| b | Byte |
| c | Character |
| d | Double |
| e | Exception |
| f | Float |
| i, j, or k | Integer |
| l | Long |
| o | Object |
| s | String |

# CHAPTER 2

# Lexical Elements

Java source code consists of words or symbols called *lexical elements*, or *tokens*. Java lexical elements include line terminators, whitespace, comments, keywords, identifiers, separators, operators, and literals. The words or symbols in the Java programming language are comprised of the Unicode character set.

## Unicode and ASCII

Maintained by the Unicode Consortium standards organization, Unicode is the universal character set with the first 128 characters the same as those in the American Standard Code for Information Interchange (ASCII) character set. Unicode provides a unique number for each character, usable across all platforms, programs, and languages. Java SE 9 supports Unicode 8.0.0. You can find more information about the Unicode Standard in the online manual (*http://www.unicode.org/versions/Unicode8.0.0/*). Java SE 8 supports Unicode 6.2.0.

The Unicode set version used by a specified version of the Java platform is documented in the Character class of the Java API. The Unicode Character Code Chart for scripts, symbols, and punctuation can be accessed at *http://unicode.org/charts/*.

## Printable ASCII Characters

ASCII reserves code 32 (spaces) and codes 33–126 (letters, digits, punctuation marks, and a few others) for printable characters. Table 2-1 contains the decimal values followed by the corresponding ASCII characters for these codes.

*Table 2-1. Printable ASCII characters*

| | | | | | | | | | | | |
|---|---|---|---|---|---|---|---|---|---|---|---|
| 32 | SP | 48 | 0 | 64 | @ | 80 | P | 96 | ' | 112 | p |
| 33 | ! | 49 | 1 | 65 | A | 81 | Q | 97 | a | 113 | q |
| 34 | " | 50 | 2 | 66 | B | 82 | R | 98 | b | 114 | r |
| 35 | # | 51 | 3 | 67 | C | 83 | S | 99 | C | 115 | S |
| 36 | $ | 52 | 4 | 68 | D | 84 | T | 100 | d | 116 | t |
| 37 | % | 53 | 5 | 69 | E | 85 | U | 101 | e | 117 | u |
| 38 | & | 54 | 6 | 70 | F | 86 | V | 102 | f | 118 | v |
| 39 | ' | 55 | 7 | 71 | G | 87 | W | 103 | g | 119 | w |
| 40 | ( | 56 | 8 | 72 | H | 88 | X | 104 | h | 120 | x |
| 41 | ) | 57 | 9 | 73 | I | 89 | Y | 105 | i | 121 | y |
| 42 | * | 58 | : | 74 | J | 90 | Z | 106 | j | 122 | z |
| 43 | + | 59 | ; | 75 | K | 91 | [ | 107 | k | 123 | { |
| 44 | , | 60 | < | 76 | L | 92 | \ | 108 | l | 124 | | |

```
45 -    61 =   77 M   93 ]   109 m   125 }
46 .    62 >   78 N   94 ^   110 n   126 ~
47 /    63 ?   79 O   95 _   111 o
```

## Nonprintable ASCII Characters

ASCII reserves decimal numbers 0–31 and 127 for *control characters*. Table 2-2 contains the decimal values followed by the corresponding ASCII characters for these codes.

*Table 2-2. Nonprintable ASCII characters*

```
00 NUL   07 BEL   14 SO    21 NAK   28 FS
01 SOH   08 BS    15 SI    22 SYN   29 GS
02 STX   09 HT    16 DLE   23 ETB   30 RS
03 ETX   10 NL    17 DC1   24 CAN   31 US
04 EOT   11 VT    18 DC2   25 EM    127 DEL
05 ENQ   12 NP    19 DC3   26 SUB
06 ACK   13 CR    20 DC4   27 ESC
```

---

#### TIP

ASCII 10 is a newline or linefeed. ASCII 13 is a carriage return.

---

# Compact Strings

The compact strings feature is an optimization that allows for a more space-efficient internal representation of strings. It is enabled by default in Java 9. This feature may be disabled by using -XX:-CompactStrings, if you are mainly using UTF-16 strings.

# Comments

A single-line comment begins with two forward slashes and ends immediately before the line terminator character:

```
// Default child's birth year
private Integer childsBirthYear = 1950;
```

A multiline comment begins with a forward slash immediately followed by an asterisk and ends with an asterisk immediately followed by a forward slash. The single asterisks in between provide a nice formatting convention; they are typically used, but are not required:

```
/*
 * The average age of a woman giving birth in the
 * US in 2001 was 24.9 years old. Therefore,
 * we'll use the value of 25 years old as our
 * default.
 */
private Integer mothersAgeGivingBirth = 25;
```

A Javadoc comment is processed by the Javadoc tool to generate API documentation in HTML format. A Javadoc comment must begin with a forward slash, immediately followed by two asterisks, and end with an asterisk immediately followed by a forward slash (Oracle's documentation page (*http://bit.ly/16mhGeT*) provides more information on the Javadoc tool):

```
/**
 * Genitor birthdate predictor
 *
 * @author Robert J. Liguori
 * @author Gliesian, LLC.
 * @version 0.1.1 09-02-16
 * @since 0.1.0 09-01-16
 */
public class GenitorBirthdatePredictorBean {...}
```

In Java, comments cannot be nested:

```
/* This is /* not permissible */ in Java */
```

# Keywords

Table 2-3 contains the Java 9 keywords. Two of these, the const and goto keywords, are reserved but are not used by the Java language.

---

**TIP**

Java keywords cannot be used as identifiers in a Java program.

---

*Table 2-3. Java keywords*

| | | | |
|---|---|---|---|
| abstract | enum | module | synchronized |
| assert | exports | native | this |
| boolean | extends | new | throw |
| break | final | package | throws |
| byte | finally | private | to |
| case | float | protected | transient |
| catch | for | provides | try |
| char | goto | public | uses |
| class | if | requires | void |
| const | implements | return | volatile |
| continue | import | short | while |
| default | instanceof | static | with |
| do | int | strictfp | _ |
| double | interface | super | |
| else | long | switch | |

# Identifiers

A Java identifier is the name that a programmer gives to a class, method, variable, and so on.

Identifiers cannot have the same Unicode character sequence as any keyword, boolean, or null literal.

Java identifiers are made up of Java letters. A Java letter is a character for which `Character.isJavaIdentifierStart(int)` returns `true`. Java letters from the ASCII character set are limited to the dollar sign (`$`), upper- and lowercase letters, and the underscore symbol (`_`). Note that as of Java 9, (`_`) is a keyword and may not be used alone as an identifier.

Digits are also allowed in identifiers *after* the first character:

```
// Valid identifier examples
class GedcomBean {
  private File uploadedFile;  // uppercase and
                              // lowercase
  private File _file; // leading underscore
  private File $file; // leading $
  private File file1; // non-leading digit
}
```

See Chapter 1 for naming guidelines.

# Separators

Several ASCII characters delimit program parts and are used as separators. `()`, `{ }`, `[ ]`, and `< >` are used in pairs:

```
() { } [ ] < > :: : ; , . ->
```

---

Table 2-4 cites nomenclature that can be used to reference the different types of bracket separators. The first names mentioned for each bracket are what is typically seen in the Java Language Specification.

*Table 2-4. Java bracket separators*

| Brackets | Nomenclature | Usage |
|---|---|---|
| ( ) | Parentheses, curved brackets, oval brackets, and round brackets | Adjusts precedence in arithmetic expressions, encloses cast types, and surrounds set of method arguments |
| { } | Braces, curly brackets, fancy brackets, squiggly brackets, and squirrelly brackets | Surrounds blocks of code and supports arrays |
| [ ] | Box brackets, closed brackets, and square brackets | Supports and initializes arrays |
| < > | Angle brackets, diamond brackets, and chevrons | Encloses generics |

Guillemet characters, a.k.a. angle quotes, are used to specify stereotypes in UML << >>.

# Operators

Operators perform operations on one, two, or three operands and return a result. Operator types in Java include assignment, arithmetic, comparison, bitwise, increment/decrement, and class/object. Table 2-5 contains the Java operators listed in precedence order (those with the highest precedence at the top of the table), along with a brief description of the operators and their associativity (left to right or right to left).

*Table 2-5. Java operators*

| Precedence | Operator | Description | Association |
|---|---|---|---|
| 1 | ++,-- | Postincrement, postdecrement | R → L |
| 2 | ++,-- | Preincrement, predecrement | R → L |
| | +,- | Unary plus, unary minus | R → L |
| | ~ | Bitwise complement | R → L |
| | ! | Boolean NOT | R → L |
| 3 | new | Create object | R → L |
| | (type) | Type cast | R → L |
| 4 | *,/,% | Multiplication, division, remainder | L → R |
| 5 | +,- | Addition, subtraction | L → R |
| | + | String concatenation | L → R |
| 6 | <<,>>,>>> | Left shift, right shift, unsigned right shift | L → R |
| 7 | <, <=, >, >= | Less than, less than or equal to, greater than, greater than or equal to | L → R |
| | instanceof | Type comparison | L → R |
| 8 | ==, != | Value equality and inequality | L → R |
| | ==, != | Reference equality and inequality | L → R |
| 9 | & | Boolean AND | L → R |
| | & | Bitwise AND | L → R |
| 10 | ^ | Boolean exclusive OR (XOR) | L → R |
| | ^ | Bitwise exclusive OR (XOR) | L → R |
| 11 | \| | Boolean inclusive OR | L → R |
| | \| | Bitwise inclusive OR | L → R |

| Precedence | Operator | Description | Association |
|---|---|---|---|
| 12 | && | Logical AND (a.k.a. conditional AND) | L → R |
| 13 | \|\| | Logical OR (a.k.a. conditional OR) | L → R |
| 14 | ?: | Conditional ternary operator | L → R |
| 15 | =, +=, -=, *=, /=, %=, &=, ^=, \|=, <<=, >> =, >>>= | Assignment operators | R → L |

# Literals

Literals are source code representation of values. As of Java SE 7, underscores are allowed in numeric literals to enhance readability of the code. The underscores may only be placed between individual numbers and are ignored at runtime.

For more information on primitive type literals, see "Literals for Primitive Types" on page 24 in Chapter 3.

## Boolean Literals

Boolean literals are expressed as either true or false:

```
boolean isFullRelation = true;
boolean isHalfRelation = Boolean.val
ueOf(false); // unboxed
boolean isEndogamyPresent = false;
```

## Character Literals

A character literal is either a single character or an escape sequence contained within single quotes. Line terminators are not allowed:

```
char charValue1 = 'a';
// An apostrophe
Character charValue2 = Character.valueOf('\'');
```

## Integer Literals

Integer types (byte, short, int, and long) can be expressed in decimal, hexadecimal, octal, and binary. By default, integer literals are of type int:

```
int intValue1 = 34567, intValue2 = 1_000_000;
```

Decimal integers contain any number of ASCII digits, zero through nine, and represent positive numbers:

```
Integer integerValue1 = Integer.valueOf(100);
```

Prefixing the decimal with the unary negation operator can form a negative decimal:

```
public static final int INT_VALUE = -200;
```

Hexadecimal literals begin with 0x or 0X, followed by the ASCII digits 0 through 9 and the letters a through f (or A through F). Java is *not* case-sensitive when it comes to hexadecimal literals.

Hex numbers can represent positive and negative integers and zero:

```
int intValue3 = 0X64; // 100 decimal from hex
```

Octal literals begin with a zero followed by one or more ASCII digits zero through seven:

```
int intValue4 = 0144; // 100 decimal from octal
```

Binary literals are expressed using the prefix 0b or 0B followed by zeros and ones:

```
char msgValue1 = 0b01001111; // O
char msgValue2 = 0B01001011; // K
char msgValue3 = 0B0010_0001; // !
```

To define an integer as type long, suffix it with an ASCII letter L (preferred and more readable) or l:

```
long longValue = 100L;
```

---

## Floating-Point Literals

A valid floating-point literal requires a whole number and/or a fractional part, decimal point, and type suffix. An exponent prefaced by an e or E is optional. Fractional parts and decimals are not required when exponents or type suffixes are applied.

A floating-point literal (double) is a double-precision floating point of eight bytes. A float is four bytes. Type suffixes for doubles are d or D; suffixes for floats are f or F:

```
[whole-number].[fractional_part][e|E exp][f|F|d|D]

float floatValue1 = 9.15f, floatValue2 = 1_168f;
Float floatValue3 = new Float(20F);
double doubleValue1 = 3.12;
Double doubleValue2 = Double.valueOf(1e058);
float expValue1 = 10.0e2f, expValue2=10.0E3f;
```

## String Literals

String literals contain zero or more characters, including escape sequences enclosed in a set of double quotes. String literals cannot contain Unicode \u000a and \u000d for line terminators; use \r and \n instead. Strings are immutable:

```
String stringValue1 = new String("Valid literal.");
String stringValue2 = "Valid.\nOn new line.";
String stringValue3 = "Joins str" + "ings";
String stringValue4 = "\"Escape Sequences\"\r";
```

There is a pool of strings associated with class String. Initially, the pool is empty. Literal strings and string-valued constant expressions are interned in the pool and added to the pool only once.

The following example shows how literals are added to and used in the pool:

```
// Adds String "thisString" to the pool
String stringValue5 = "thisString";
```

```
// Uses String "thisString" from the pool
String stringValue6 = "thisString";
```

A string can be added to the pool (if it does not already exist in the pool) by calling the intern() method on the string. The intern() method returns a string, which is either a reference to the new string that was added to the pool or a reference to the existing string:

```
String stringValue7 = new String("thatString");
String stringValue8 = stringValue7.intern();
```

## Null Literals

The null literal is of type null and can be applied to reference types. It does not apply to primitive types:

```
String n = null;
```

# Escape Sequences

Table 2-6 provides the set of escape sequences in Java.

*Table 2-6. Character and string literal escape sequences*

| Name | Sequence | Decimal | Unicode |
|---|---|---|---|
| Backspace | \b | 8 | \u0008 |
| Horizontal tab | \t | 9 | \u0009 |
| Line feed | \n | 10 | \u000A |
| Form feed | \f | 12 | \u000C |
| Carriage return | \r | 13 | \u000D |
| Double quote | \" | 34 | \u0022 |
| Single quote | \' | 39 | \u0027 |

Different line terminators are used for different platforms to achieve a newline (see Table 2-7). The println() method, which includes a line break, is a better solution than hardcoding \n and \r when used appropriately.

*Table 2-7. Newline variations*

| Operating system | Newline |
|---|---|
| POSIX-compliant operating systems (e.g., Solaris, Linux) and macOS | LF (\n) |
| Microsoft Windows | CR+LF (\r\n) |
| macOS up to version 9 | CR (\r) |

## Unicode Currency Symbols

Unicode currency symbols are present in the range of \u20A0–\u20CF (8352–8399). See Table 2-8 for examples.

*Table 2-8. Currency symbols within range*

| Name | Symbol | Decimal | Unicode |
|---|---|---|---|
| Franc sign | ₣ | 8355 | \u20A3 |
| Lira sign | ₤ | 8356 | \u20A4 |
| Mill sign | ₥ | 8357 | \u20A5 |
| Rupee sign | ₨ | 8360 | \u20A8 |
| Dong sign | ₫ | 8363 | \u20AB |
| Euro sign | € | 8364 | \u20AC |
| Drachma sign | ₯ | 8367 | \u20AF |
| German penny sign | ₰ | 8368 | \u20B0 |

A number of currency symbols exist outside of the designated currency range. See Table 2-9 for examples.

*Table 2-9. Currency symbols outside of range*

| Name | Symbol | Decimal | Unicode |
|------|--------|---------|---------|
| Dollar sign | $ | 36 | \u0024 |
| Cent sign | ¢ | 162 | \u00A2 |
| Pound sign | £ | 163 | \u00A3 |
| Currency sign | ¤ | 164 | \u00A4 |
| Yen sign | ¥ | 165 | \u00A5 |
| Latin small f with hook | ƒ | 402 | \u0192 |
| Bengali rupee mark | ৲ | 2546 | \u09F2 |
| Bengali rupee sign | ৳ | 2547 | \u09F3 |
| Gujarati rupee sign | ૱ | 2801 | \u0AF1 |
| Tamil rupee sign | ௹ | 3065 | \u0BF9 |
| Thai symbol baht | ฿ | 3647 | \u0E3F |
| Script captial | ℳ | 8499 | \u2133 |
| CJK unified ideograph 1 | 元 | 20803 | \u5143 |
| CJK unified ideograph 2 | 円 | 20870 | \u5186 |
| CJK unified ideograph 3 | 圆 | 22278 | \u5706 |
| CJK unified ideograph 4 | 圓 | 22291 | \u5713 |

# CHAPTER 3

# Fundamental Types

Fundamental types include the Java primitive types and their corresponding wrapper classes/reference types. There is provision for automatic conversion between these primitive and reference types through autoboxing and unboxing. Numeric promotion is applied to primitive types where appropriate.

## Primitive Types

There are eight primitive types in Java: each is a reserved keyword. They describe variables that contain single values of the appropriate format and size (see Table 3-1). Primitive types are always the specified precision, regardless of the underlying hardware precisions (e.g., 32- or 64-bit).

*Table 3-1. Primitive types*

| Type | Detail | Storage | Range |
|------|--------|---------|-------|
| boolean | true or false | 1 bit | Not applicable |
| char | Unicode character | 2 bytes | \u0000 to \uFFFF |
| byte | Integer | 1 byte | −128 to 127 |
| short | Integer | 2 bytes | −32768 to 32767 |
| int | Integer | 4 bytes | −2147483648 to 2147483647 |

| Type | Detail | Storage | Range |
|------|--------|---------|-------|
| long | Integer | 8 bytes | $-2^{63}$ to $2^{63}-1$ |
| float | Floating point | 4 bytes | $1.4e^{-45}$ to $3.4e^{+38}$ |
| double | Floating point | 8 bytes | $5e^{-324}$ to $1.8e^{+308}$ |

---

### TIP

Primitive types byte, short, int, long, float, and double are all signed. Type char is unsigned.

---

## Literals for Primitive Types

All primitive types except boolean can accept character, decimal, hexadecimal, octal, and Unicode literal formats, as well as character escape sequences. Where appropriate, the literal value is automatically cast or converted. Remember that bits are lost during truncation. The following is a list of primitive assignment examples.

The boolean primitive's only valid literal values are true and false:

```
boolean isEndogamous = true;
```

The char primitive represents a single Unicode character. Literal values of the char primitive that are greater than two bytes need to be explicitly cast.

```
// 'atDNA'
  char[] cArray = {
  '\'', // '
  '\u0061', // a
  't', // t
  0x0044, // D
  0116, // N
  (char) (65 + 131072) , // A
  0b00100111}; // '
```

The `byte` primitive has a four-byte signed integer as its valid literal. If an explicit cast is not performed, the integer is implicitly cast to one byte:

```
final byte CHROMOSOME_PAIRS = 12;
final byte CHROMOSOME_TOTAL = (byte) 48;
```

The `short` primitive has a four-byte signed integer as its valid literal. If an explicit cast is not performed, the integer is implicitly cast to two bytes:

```
short firstCousins = 6;
short secondCousins = (short) 18;
```

The `int` primitive has a four-byte signed integer as its valid literal. When `char`, `byte`, and `short` primitives are used as literals, they are automatically cast to four-byte integers, as in the case of the `short` value within `vipSeats`. Floating-point and long literals must be explicitly cast:

```
int thirdCousins = 104;
int forthCousins = (int) 648.0D;
int fifthCousins = (short) 3_888;
```

The `long` primitive has an eight-byte signed integer as its valid literal. It is designated by an L or l postfix. The value is cast from four bytes to eight bytes when no postfix or cast is applied:

```
long sixthCousins = 23_000;
long seventhCousins = (long) 138_000;
long eighthCousins = 828_000l;
long ninthCousins = 4_968_000L;
```

The `float` primitive has a four-byte signed floating point as its valid literal. An F or f postfix or an explicit cast designates it. Even though no explicit cast is necessary for an `int` literal, an `int` will not always fit into a `float` where the value exceeds about $2^{23}$:

```
float totalSharedCentimorgansX = 0;
float totalSharedCentimorgansAutosomal = (float)
285.5;
```

```
float largestSharedCentimorgansX = 0.0f;
float largestSharedCentimorgansAutosomal = 71F;
```

The double primitive uses an eight-byte signed floating-point value as its valid literal. The literal can have a D, d, or explicit cast with no postfix. If the literal is an integer, it is implicitly cast:

```
double centimorgansSharedFloor = 0;
double centimorgansSharedCeiling = 6766.20;
double centimorgansShared = (double) 888;
double centimorgansUnShared = 5878.0d;
double centimorgansPercentShared = 13.12D;
```

See Chapter 2 for more details on literals.

# Floating-Point Entities

Positive and negative floating-point infinities, negative zero, and *not a number* (NaN) are special entities defined to meet the IEEE 754-1985 standard (see Table 3-2).

The Infinity, -Infinity, and -0.0 entities are returned when an operation creates a floating-point value that is too large to be traditionally represented.

*Table 3-2. Floating-point entities*

| Entity | Description | Examples |
| --- | --- | --- |
| Infinity | Represents the concept of positive infinity | 1.0 / 0.0, 1e300 / 1e−300, Math.abs (−1.0 / 0.0) |
| -Infinity | Represents the concept of negative infinity | −1.0 / 0.0, 1.0 / (−0.0), 1e300/−1e−300 |
| -0.0 | Represents a negative number close to zero | −1.0 / (1.0 / 0.0), −1e−300 / 1e300 |
| NaN | Represents undefined results | 0.0 / 0.0, 1e300 * Float.NaN, Math.sqrt (−9.0) |

Positive infinity, negative infinity, and NaN entities are available as double and float constants:

```
Double.POSITIVE_INFINITY; // Infinity
Float.POSITIVE_INFINITY;  // Infinity
Double.NEGATIVE_INFINITY; // -Infinity
Float.NEGATIVE_INFINITY;  // -Infinity
Double.NaN; // Not-a-Number
Float.NaN;  // Not-a-Number
```

The Double and Float wrapper classes have methods to determine if a number is finite, infinite, or NaN:

```
Double.isFinite(Double.POSITIVE_INFINITY); // false
Double.isFinite(Double.NEGATIVE_INFINITY); // false
Double.isFinite(Double.NaN); // false
Double.isFinite(1); // true
// true
Double.isInfinite(Double.POSITIVE_INFINITY);
// true
Double.isInfinite(Double.NEGATIVE_INFINITY);
Double.isInfinite(Double.NaN); // false
Double.isInfinite(1); // false
Double.isNaN(Double.NaN); // true
Double.isNaN(1); // false
```

## Operations Involving Special Entities

Table 3-3 shows the results of special entity operations where the operands are abbreviated as INF for Double.POSITIVE_INFIN ITY, -INF for Double.NEGATIVE_INFINITY, and NAN for Dou ble.NaN.

For example, column 4's heading entry (–0.0) and row 12's entry (\* NAN) have a result of NaN, and could be written as follows:

```
// 'NaN' will be printed
System.out.print((-0.0) * Double.NaN);
```

Table 3-3. Operations involving special entities

|          | INF       | (−INF)    | (−0.0)    |
|----------|-----------|-----------|-----------|
| *INF     | Infinity  | -Infinity | NaN       |
| +INF     | Infinity  | NaN       | Infinity  |
| −INF     | NaN       | -Infinity | -Infinity |
| /INF     | NaN       | NaN       | -0.0      |
| *0.0     | NaN       | NaN       | -0.0      |
| +0.0     | Infinity  | -Infinity | 0.0       |
| +0.5     | Infinity  | -Infinity | 0.5       |
| *0.5     | Infinity  | -Infinity | -0.0      |
| +(−0.5)  | Infinity  | -Infinity | -0.5      |
| *(−0.5)  | -Infinity | Infinity  | 0.0       |
| +NAN     | NaN       | NaN       | NaN       |
| *NAN     | NaN       | NaN       | NaN       |

**TIP**

Any operation performed on NaN results in NaN; there is no such thing as -NaN.

# Numeric Promotion of Primitive Types

Numeric promotion consists of rules that are applied to the operands of an arithmetic operator under certain conditions. Numeric promotion rules consist of both unary and binary promotion rules.

## Unary Numeric Promotion

When a primitive of a numeric type is part of an expression, as listed in Table 3-4, the following promotion rules are applied:

- If the operand is of type byte, short, or char, the type will be promoted to type int.

- Otherwise, the type of the operand remains unchanged.

*Table 3-4. Expression for unary promotion rules*

| Expression |
| --- |
| Operand of a unary plus operator |
| Operand of a unary minus operator − |
| Operand of a bitwise complement operator ~ |
| All shift operators >>, >>>, or << |
| Index expression in an array access expression |
| Dimension expression in an array creation expression |

## Binary Numeric Promotion

When two primitives of different numerical types are compared via the operators listed in Table 3-5, one type is promoted based on the following binary promotion rules:

- If either operand is of type double, the non-double primitive is converted to type double.

- If either operand is of type float, the non-float primitive is converted to type float.

- If either operand is of type long, the non-long primitive is converted to type long.

- Otherwise, both operands are converted to int.

*Table 3-5. Operators for binary promotion rules*

| Operators | Description |
|---|---|
| + and − | Additive operators |
| *, /, and % | Multiplicative operators |
| <, <=, >, and >= | Comparison operators |
| == and != | Equality operators |
| &, ^, and \| | Bitwise operators |
| ? : | Conditional operator (see next section) |

## Special Cases for Conditional Operators

- If one operand is of type byte and the other is of type short, the conditional expression will be of type short:

    ```
    short = true ? byte : short
    ```

- If one operand *R* is of type byte, short, or char, and the other is a constant expression of type int whose value is within range of *R*, the conditional expression is of type *R*:

    ```
    short = (true ? short : 1967)
    ```

- Otherwise, binary numeric promotion is applied, and the conditional expression type will be that of the promoted type of the second and third operands.

# Wrapper Classes

Each of the primitive types has a corresponding wrapper class/reference type, which is located in package java.lang. Each wrapper class has a variety of methods, including one to return the type's value, as shown in Table 3-6. These integer and floating-point wrapper classes can return values of several primitive types.

*Table 3-6. Wrapper classes*

| Primitive types | Reference types | Methods to get primitive values |
|---|---|---|
| boolean | Boolean | booleanValue() |
| char | Character | charValue() |
| byte | Byte | byteValue(), shortValue(), intValue(), longValue(), float Value(), doubleValue() |
| short | Short | byteValue(), shortValue(), intValue(), longValue(), float Value(), doubleValue() |
| int | Integer | byteValue(), shortValue(), intValue(), longValue(), float Value(), doubleValue() |
| long | Long | byteValue(), shortValue(), intValue(), longValue(), float Value(), doubleValue() |
| float | Float | byteValue(), shortValue(), intValue(), longValue(), float Value(), doubleValue() |
| double | Double | byteValue(), shortValue(), intValue(), longValue(), float Value(), doubleValue() |

# Autoboxing and Unboxing

Autoboxing and unboxing are typically used for collections of primitives. Autoboxing involves the dynamic allocation of memory and the initialization of an object for each primitive. Note that the overhead can often exceed the execution time of the desired operation. Unboxing involves the production of a primitive for each object.

Computationally intensive tasks using primitives (e.g., iterating through primitives in a container) should be done using arrays of primitives instead of collections of wrapper objects.

## Autoboxing

Autoboxing is the automatic conversion of primitive types to their corresponding wrapper classes. In this example, the diploid chromosome number for each species (e.g., 60, 46, and 38) are automatically converted to their corresponding wrappers class because collections store references, not primitive values:

```
// Create hash map of weight groups
HashMap<String, Integer> diploidChromosomeNumberMap
    = new HashMap<String, Integer> ();
diploidChromosomeNumberMap.put("Canis latrans",
78);
diploidChromosomeNumberMap.put("Bison bison", 60);
diploidChromosomeNumberMap.put("Homo sapiens", 46);
diploidChromosomeNumberMap.put("Sus scrofa", 38);
diploidChromosomeNumberMap.put("Myrmecia pilo
sula", 2);
```

The following example shows an acceptable but not recommended use of autoboxing:

```
// Set number of autosomal (atDNA) chromosomes
Integer atDnaChromosomeSet = 22; //improper
```

As there is no reason to force autoboxing, the preceding statement should instead be written as follows:

```
Integer atDnaChromosomeSet = Integer.valueOf(22);
```

## Unboxing

Unboxing is the automatic conversion of the wrapper classes to their corresponding primitive types. In this example, a reference type is retrieved from the hash map. It is automatically unboxed so that it can fit into the primitive type:

```
// Get the DCN of a homo sapien, performing unbox
ing
int homoSapienDcn = diploidChromosomeNumber
Map.get("Homo sapiens");

System.out.println(homoSapienDcn);
$ 46
```

The following example shows an acceptable but not recommended use of unboxing:

```
// Establish the total number of chromosomes
Integer atDnaChromosomeSet = 22;
int multiplier = 2;
int xChromosomes = 2; // 1 or 2
int yChromosome = 0;   // 0 or 1
// Mixing int and Integer; not recommended
int dcn = xChromosomes + yChromosome
   + (multiplier * atDnaChromosomeSet);
```

It is better to write this expression with the intValue() method,
as shown here:

```
int dcn = xChromosomes + yChromosome
   + (multiplier * atDnaChromosomeSet.intValue());
```

# CHAPTER 4

# Reference Types

Reference types hold references to objects and provide a means to access those objects stored somewhere in memory. The memory locations are irrelevant to programmers. All reference types are a subclass of type `java.lang.Object`.

Table 4-1 lists the five Java reference types.

*Table 4-1. Reference types*

| Reference type | Brief description |
|---|---|
| Annotation | Provides a way to associate metadata (data about data) with program elements. |
| Array | Provides a fixed-size data structure that stores data elements of the same type. |
| Class | Designed to provide inheritance, polymorphism, and encapsulation. Usually models something in the real world and consists of a set of values that holds data and a set of methods that operates on the data. |
| Enumeration | A reference for a set of objects that represents a related set of choices. |
| Interface | Provides a public API and is "implemented" by Java classes. |

# Comparing Reference Types to Primitive Types

There are two type categories in Java: reference types and primitive types. Table 4-2 shows some of the key differences between them. See Chapter 3 for more details.

*Table 4-2. Reference types compared with primitive types*

| Reference types | Primitive types |
| --- | --- |
| Unlimited number of reference types, as they are defined by the user. | Consists of `boolean` and numeric types: `char`, `byte`, `short`, `int`, `long`, `float`, and `double`. |
| Memory location stores a reference to the data. | Memory location stores actual data held by the primitive type. |
| When a reference type is assigned to another reference type, both will point to the same object. | When a value of a primitive is assigned to another variable of the same type, a copy is made. |
| When an object is passed into a method, the called method can change the contents of the object passed to it but not the address of the object. | When a primitive is passed into a method, only a copy of the primitive is passed. The called method does not have access to the original primitive value and therefore cannot change it. The called method can change the copied value. |

# Default Values

Default values are the values assigned to instance variables in Java, when no initialization value has been explicitly set.

## Instance and Local Variable Objects

Instance variables (i.e., those declared at the class level) have a default value of `null`. `null` references nothing.

Local variables (i.e., those declared within a method) do not have a default value, not even a value of `null`. Always initialize local variables because they are not given a default value.

Checking an uninitialized local variable object for a value (including a value of null) will result in a compile-time error.

Although object references with a value of null do not refer to any object on the heap, objects set to null can be referenced in code *without* receiving compile-time or runtime errors:

```
LocalDate birthdate = null;
// This will compile
if (birthdate == null) {
  System.out.println(birthdate);
}
$ null
```

Invoking a method on a reference variable that is null or using the dot operator on the object will result in a java.lang.Null PointerException:

```
final int MAX_LENGTH = 20;
String partyTheme = null;
/*
 * java.lang.NullPointerException is thrown
 * since partyTheme is null
 */
if (partyTheme.length() > MAX_LENGTH) {}
```

## Arrays

Arrays are always given a default value whether they are declared as instance variables or local variables. Arrays that are declared but not initialized are given a default value of null.

In the following code, the gameList1 array is initialized, but not the individual values, meaning that the object references will have a value of null. Objects have to be added to the array:

```
/*
 * The declared arrays named gameList1 and
 * gameList2 are initialized to null by default
 */
Game[] gameList1;
Game gameList2[];
```

```
/*
 * The following array has been initialized but
 * the object references are still null because
 * the array contains no objects
 */
   gameList1 = new Game[10];

// Add a Game object to the list, so it has one
object
   gameList1[0] = new Game();
```

Multidimensional arrays in Java are actually arrays of arrays.
They may be initialized with the new operator or by placing
their values within braces. Multidimensional arrays may be
uniform or nonuniform in shape:

```
// Anonymous array
int twoDimensionalArray[][] = new int[6][6];
twoDimensionalArray[0][0] = 100;
int threeDimensionalArray[][][] = new int[2][2][2];
threeDimensionalArray[0][0][0] = 200;
int varDimensionArray[][] = {{0,0},{1,1,1},
{2,2,2,2}};
varDimensionArray[0][0] = 300;
```

Anonymous arrays allow for the creation of a new array of values anywhere in the code base:

```
// Examples using anonymous arrays
int[] luckyNumbers = new int[] {7, 13, 21};
int totalWinnings = sum(new int[] {3000, 4500,
5000});
```

# Conversion of Reference Types

An object can be converted to the type of its superclass (widening) or any of its subclasses (narrowing).

The compiler checks conversions at compile time, and the *Java
Virtual Machine* (JVM) checks conversions at runtime.

# Widening Conversions

- Widening implicitly converts a subclass to a parent class (superclass).
- Widening conversions do not throw runtime exceptions.
- No explicit cast is necessary:

```
String s = new String();
Object o = s; // widening
```

# Narrowing Conversions

- Narrowing converts a more general type into a more specific type.
- Narrowing is a conversion of a superclass to a subclass.
- An explicit cast is required. To cast an object to another object, place the type of object to which you are casting in parentheses immediately before the object you are casting.
- Illegitimate narrowing results in a ClassCastException.
- Narrowing may result in a loss of data/precision.

Objects cannot be converted to an unrelated type—that is, a type other than one of its subclasses or superclasses. Doing so will generate an inconvertible types error at compile time. The following is an example of a conversion that will result in a compile-time error due to inconvertible types:

```
Object o = new Object();
String s = (Integer) o;  // compile-time error
```

# Converting Between Primitives and Reference Types

The automatic conversion of primitive types to reference types, and vice versa, is called *autoboxing* and *unboxing*, respectively. For more information, refer back to Chapter 3.

# Passing Reference Types into Methods

When an object is passed into a method as a variable:

- A copy of the reference variable is passed, not the actual object.

- The caller and the called methods have identical copies of the reference.

- The caller will also see any changes the called method makes to the object. Passing a copy of the object to the called method will prevent it from making changes to the original object.

- The called method cannot change the address of the object, but it can change the contents of the object.

The following example illustrates passing reference types and primitive types into methods and the effects on those types when changed by the called method:

```
void roomSetup() {
  // Reference passing
  Table table = new Table();
  table.setLength(72);
  // Length will be changed
  modTableLength(table);

  // Primitive passing
  // Value of chairs not changed
  int chairs = 8;
  modChairCount(chairs);
}
```

```
void modTableLength(Table t) {
  t.setLength(36);
}

void modChairCount(int i) {
  i = 10;
}
```

# Comparing Reference Types

Reference types are comparable in Java. Equality operators and the equals method can be used to assist with comparisons.

## Using the Equality Operators

The != and == equality operators are used to compare the memory locations of two objects. If the memory addresses of the objects being compared are the same, the objects are considered equal. These equality operators are not used to compare the contents of two objects.

In the following example, guest1 and guest2 have the same memory address, so the statement "They are equal" is output:

```
String guest1 = new String("name");
String guest2 = guest1;
if (guest1 == guest2)
  System.out.println("They are equal");
```

In the following example, the memory addresses are not equal, so the statement "They are not equal" is output:

```
String guest1 = new String("name");
String guest2 = new String("name");
if (guest1 != guest2)
  System.out.println("They are not equal");
```

## Using the equals() Method

To compare the contents of two class objects, the equals()method from class Object can be used or overridden.

When the equals() method is overridden, the hashCode() method should also be overridden. This is done for compatibility with hash-based collections such as HashMap() and Hash Set().

---

**TIP**

By default, the equals() method uses only the == operator for comparisons. This method has to be overridden to really be useful.

---

For example, if you want to compare values contained in two instances of the same class, you should use a programmer-defined equals() method.

## Comparing Strings

There are two ways to check whether strings are equal in Java, but the definition of "equal" for each of them is different:

- The equals() method compares two strings, character by character, to determine equality. This is not the default implementation of the equals() method provided by the Object class. This is the overridden implementation provided by String class.

- The == operator checks to see whether two object references refer to the same instance of an object.

Here is a program that shows how strings are evaluated using the equals() method and the == operator (for more information on how strings are evaluated, see "String Literals" on page 19 in Chapter 2):

```
class MyComparisons {

    // Add string to pool
    String first = "chairs";
```

```
  // Use string from pool
  String second = "chairs";
  // Create a new string
  String third = new String ("chairs");

void myMethod() {

  /*
   * Contrary to popular belief, this evaluates
   * to true. Try it!
   */
  if (first == second) {
    System.out.println("first == second");
  }

  // This evaluates to true
  if (first.equals(second)) {
    System.out.println("first equals second");
  }
  // This evaluates to false
  if (first == third) {
    System.out.println("first == third");
  }
  // This evaluates to true
  if (first.equals(third)) {
    System.out.println("first equals third");
  }
} // End myMethod()
} //end class
```

---

### TIP

Objects of the StringBuffer and StringBuilder classes
are mutable. Objects of the String class are immutable.

---

## Comparing Enumerations

enum values can be compared using == or the equals() method because they return the same result. The == operator is used more frequently to compare enumeration types.

# Copying Reference Types

When reference types are copied, either a copy of the reference to an object is made, or an actual copy of the object is made, creating a new object. The latter is referred to as *cloning* in Java.

## Copying a Reference to an Object

When copying a reference to an object, the result is one object with two references. In the following example, closingSong is assigned a reference to the object pointed to by lastSong. Any changes made to lastSong will be reflected in closingSong, and vice versa:

```
Song lastSong = new Song();
Song closingSong = lastSong;
```

## Cloning Objects

Cloning results in another copy of the object, not just a copy of a reference to an object. Cloning is not available to classes by default. Note that cloning is usually very complex, so you should consider a copy constructor instead, for the following reasons:

- For a class to be cloneable, it must implement the interface Cloneable.

- The protected method clone() allows for objects to clone themselves.

- For an object to clone an object other than itself, the clone() method must be overridden and made public by the object being cloned.

- When cloning, a cast must be used because clone() returns type object.
- Cloning can throw a CloneNotSupportedException.

### Shallow and deep cloning

Shallow and deep cloning are the two types of cloning in Java.

In shallow cloning, primitive values and the references in the object being cloned are copied. Copies of the objects referred to by those references are not made.

In the following example, leadingSong will be assigned the value of length because it is a primitive type. Also, leadingSong will be assigned the references to title, artist, and year because they are references to types:

```
class Song {
  String title;
  Artist artist;
  float length;
  Year year;
  void setData() {...}
}
Song firstSong = new Song();
try {
  // Make an actual copy by cloning
  Song leadingSong = (Song)firstSong.clone();
} catch (CloneNotSupportedException cnse) {
  cnse.printStackTrace();
} // end
```

In deep cloning, the cloned object makes a copy of each of its object's fields, recursing through all other objects referenced by it. A deep-clone method must be defined by the programmer, as the Java API does not provide one. Alternatives to deep cloning are serialization and copy constructors. (Copy constructors are often preferred over serialization.)

## Memory Allocation and Garbage Collection of Reference Types

When a new object is created, memory is allocated. When there are no references to an object, the memory that object used can be reclaimed during the garbage collection process. For more information on this topic, see Chapter 11.

CHAPTER 5

# Object-Oriented Programming

Basic elements of *object-oriented programming* (OOP) in Java include classes, objects, and interfaces.

## Classes and Objects

*Classes* define entities that usually represent something in the real world. They consist of a set of values that holds data and a set of methods that operates on the data.

Classes can inherit data members and methods from other classes. A class can directly inherit from only one class—the *superclass*. A class can have only one direct superclass. This is called *inheritance*.

An instance of a class is called an *object*, and it is allocated memory. There can be multiple instances of a class.

When implementing a class, the inner details of the class should be `private` and accessible only through public interfaces. This is called *encapsulation*. The JavaBean convention is to use accessor and mutator methods (e.g., `getFirstName()` and `setFirstName("Leonardina")`) to indirectly access the private members of a class and to ensure that another class cannot unexpectedly modify private members. Returning immutable values (i.e., strings, primitive values, and objects intentionally made immutable) is another way to protect the data members from being altered by other objects.

## Class Syntax

A class has a class signature, optional constructors, data members, and methods:

```
[javaModifiers] class className
  [extends someSuperClass]
  [implements someInterfaces separated by commas] {
  // Data member(s)
  // Constructor(s)
  // Method(s)
}
```

## Instantiating a Class (Creating an Object)

An object is an instance of a class. Once instantiated, objects have their own set of data members and methods:

```
// Sample class definitions
public class Candidate {...}
class Stats extends ToolSet {...}


public class Report extends ToolSet
  implements Runnable {...}
```

Separate objects of class Candidate are created (instantiated) using the keyword new:

```
Candidate candidate1 = new Candidate();
Candidate candidate2 = new Candidate();
```

## Data Members and Methods

Data members, also known as *fields*, hold data about a class. Data members that are nonstatic are also called *instance variables*:

```
[javaModifier] type dataMemberName
```

Methods operate on class data:

```
[javaModifiers] type methodName (parameterList)
[throws listOfExceptionsSeparatedByCommas]  {
  // Method body
}
```

The following is an example of class `Candidate` and its data members and methods:

```
public class Candidate {
  // Data members or fields
  private String firstName;
  private String lastName;
  private String party;
  // Methods
  public void setParty (String p) {party = p;}
  public String getLastName() {return lastName;}
} // End class Candidate
```

## Accessing Data Members and Methods in Objects

The dot operator (.) is used to access data members and methods in objects. It is not necessary to use the dot operator when accessing data members or methods from within an object:

```
candidate1.setParty("Whig");
String name = getFirstName() + getLastName();
```

## Overloading

Methods, including constructors, can be overloaded. Overloading means that two or more methods have the same name but different signatures (parameters and return values). Note that overloaded methods must have different parameters, and they may have different return types; but having only different return types is not overloading. The access modifiers of overloaded methods can be different:

```
public class VotingMachine {
  ...
  public void startUp() {...}
```

```
    private void startUp(int delay) {...}
}
```

When a method is overloaded, it is permissible for each of its signatures to throw different checked exceptions:

```
private String startUp(District d) throws IOExcep
tion {...}
```

## Overriding

A subclass can override the methods it inherits. When overridden, a method contains the same signature (name and parameters) as a method in its superclass, but it has different implementation details.

The method startUp() in superclass Display is overridden in class TouchScreenDisplay:

```
public class Display {
  void startUp(){
    System.out.println("Using base display.");
  }
}
public class TouchScreenDisplay extends Display {
    void startUp() {
    System.out.println("Using new display.");
  }
}
```

Rules regarding overriding methods include the following:

- Methods that are not final, private, or static can be overridden.

- Protected methods can override methods that do not have access modifiers.

- The overriding method cannot have a more restrictive access modifier (i.e., package, public, private, protec ted) than the original method.

- The overriding method cannot throw any new checked exceptions.

## Constructors

Constructors are called upon object creation and are used to initialize data in the newly created object. Constructors are optional, have exactly the same name as the class, and they do not have a `return` in the body (as methods do).

A class can have multiple constructors. The constructor that is called when a new object is created is the one that has a matching signature:

```
public class Candidate {
  ...
  Candidate(int id) {
    this.identification = id;
  }
  Candidate(int id, int age) {
    this.identification = id;
    this.age = age;
  }
}
// Create a new Candidate and call its constructor
Candidate candidate = new Candidate(id);
```

Classes implicitly have a no-argument constructor if no explicit constructor is present. Note that if a constructor with arguments is added, there will be no no-argument constructor unless it is manually added.

## Superclasses and Subclasses

In Java, a class (known as the *subclass*) can inherit directly from one class (known as the *superclass*). The Java keyword `extends` indicates that a class inherits data members and methods from another class. Subclasses do not have direct access to `private` members of its superclass, but do have access to the `public` and `protected` members of the superclass. A subclass also has access to members of the superclass where the same package is shared (*package-private* or protected). As previously mentioned, accessor and mutator methods provide a mechanism to indirectly access the private members of a class, including a superclass:

```
public class Machine {
  boolean state;
  void setState(boolean s) {state = s;}
  boolean getState() {return state;}
}
public class VotingMachine extends Machine {
  ...
}
```

The keyword super is used to access methods in the superclass overridden by methods in the subclass:

```
public class PrivacyWall {
  public void printSpecs() {
    System.out.println("Printed PrivacyWall
Specs");
  }
}
public class Curtain extends PrivacyWall {
  public void printSpecs() {
    super.printSpecs();
    System.out.println("Printed Curtain Specs");
  }
  public static void main(String[] args) {
    Curtain curtain = new Curtain();
    curtain.printSpecs();
  }
}
$ Printed PrivacyWall Specs
$ Printed Curtain Specs
```

Another common use of the keyword super is to call the constructor of a superclass and pass it parameters. Note that this call must be the first statement in the constructor calling super:

```
public PrivacyWall(int length, int width) {
  this.length = length;
  this.width = width;
  this.area = length * width;
}

public class Curtain extends PrivacyWall {
  // Set default length and width
  public Curtain()  {super(15, 25);}
}
```

If there is not an explicit call to the constructor of the super-class, an automatic call to the no-argument constructor of the superclass is made.

## The this Keyword

The three common uses of the this keyword are to refer to the current object, to call a constructor from within another constructor in the same class, and to pass a reference of the current object to another object.

To assign a parameter variable to an instance variable of the current object:

```
public class Curtain extends PrivacyWall {
  String color;
  public void setColor(String color) {
    this.color = color;
  }
}
```

To call a constructor from another constructor in the same class:

```
public class Curtain extends PrivacyWall {
  public Curtain(int length, int width) {}
  public Curtain() {this(10, 9);}
}
```

To pass a reference of the current object to another object:

```
// Print the contents of class curtain
System.out.println(this);
```

```
public class Builder {
  public void setWallType(Curtain c) {...}
}
```

# Variable-Length Argument Lists

Methods can have a variable-length argument list. Called *varargs*, these methods are declared such that the last (and only the last) argument can be repeated zero or more times when the method is called. The vararg parameter can be either a primitive or an object. An ellipsis (...) is used in the argument list of the method signature to declare the method as a vararg. The syntax of the vararg parameter is as follows:

```
type... objectOrPrimitiveName
```

Here is an example of a signature for a vararg method:

```
public setDisplayButtons(int row,
  String... names) {...}
```

The Java compiler modifies vararg methods to look like regular methods. The previous example would be modified at compile time to:

```
public setDisplayButtons(int row,
  String [] names) {...}
```

It is permissible for a vararg method to have a vararg parameter as its only parameter:

```
// Zero or more rows
public void setDisplayButtons (String... names)
{...}
```

A vararg method is called the same way that an ordinary method is called except that it can take a variable number of parameters, repeating only the last argument:

---

```
setDisplayButtons("Jim");
setDisplayButtons("John", "Mary", "Pete");
setDisplayButtons("Sue", "Doug", "Terry", "John");
```

The printf method is often used when formatting a variable set of output, because printf is a vararg method. From the Java API, type the following:

```
public PrintStream printf(String format,
    Object... args)
```

The printf method is called with a format string and a variable set of objects:

```
System.out.printf("Hello voter %s%n
    This is machine %d%n", "Sally", 1);
```

For detailed information on formatting a string passed into the printf method, see java.util.Formatter.

The enhanced for loop (for each) is often used to iterate through the variable argument:

```
printRows() {
    for (String name: names)
        System.out.println(name);
}
```

# Abstract Classes and Abstract Methods

Abstract classes and methods are declared with the keyword abstract.

## Abstract Classes

An abstract class is typically used as a base class and cannot be instantiated. It can contain abstract and nonabstract methods, and it can be a subclass of an abstract or a nonabstract class. All of its abstract methods must be defined by the classes that inherit (extend) it unless the subclass is also abstract:

```
public abstract class Alarm {
    public void reset() {...}
```

```
  public abstract void renderAlarm();
}
```

## Abstract Methods

An abstract method contains only the method declaration,
which must be defined by any nonabstract class that inherits it:

```
public class DisplayAlarm extends Alarm {
  public void renderAlarm() {
    System.out.println("Active alarm.");
  }
}
```

# Static Data Members, Static Methods, Static Constants, and Static Initializers

Static data members, methods, constants, and initializers reside
with a class and not instances of classes. Static data members,
methods, and constants can be accessed in the class in which
they are defined or in another class using the dot operator.

## Static Data Members

Static data members have the same features as static methods
and are stored in a single location in memory.

They are used when only one copy of a data member is needed
across all instances of a class (e.g., a counter):

```
// Declaring a static data member
public class Voter  {
  static int voterCount = 0;
  public Voter() { voterCount++;}
  public static int getVoterCount() {
    return voterCount;
  }
}
...
int numVoters = Voter.voterCount;
```

## Static Methods

Static methods have the keyword static in the method declaration:

```
// Declaring a static method
class Analyzer {
  public static int getVotesByAge() {...}
}
// Using the static method
Analyzer.getVotesByAge();
```

Static methods cannot access nonstatic methods or variables because static methods are associated with a class, not an object.

## Static Constants

Static constants are static members declared constant. They have the keywords static and final, and a program cannot change them:

```
// Declaring a static constant
static final int AGE_LIMIT = 18;
// Using a static constant
if (age == AGE_LIMIT)
  newVoter = "yes";
```

## Static Initializers

Static initializers include a block of code prefaced by the keyword static. A class can have any number of static initializer blocks, and it is guaranteed that they will run in the order in which they appear. Static initializer blocks are executed only once per class initialization. A block is run when the JVM class loader loads StaticClass, which is upon the initial reference to the code:

```
public class Election {
  private static int numberOfCandidates;
  // Static Initializer
  static {
```

```
      numberOfCandidates = getNumberOfCandidates();
  }
}
```

# Interfaces

Interfaces provide a set of declared public methods that do not
have method bodies. A class that implements an interface must
provide concrete implementations of all the methods defined
by the interface, or it must be declared abstract.

An interface is declared using the keyword interface, followed
by the name of the interface and a set of method declarations.

Interface names are usually adjectives and end with "able" or
"ible," as the interface provides a capability:

```
interface Reportable  {
  void genReport(String repType);
  void printReport(String repType);
}
```

A class that implements an interface must indicate so in its
class signature with the keyword implements:

```
class VotingMachine implements Reportable {
  public void genReport (String repType) {
    Report report = new Report(repType);
  }
  public void printReport(String repType) {
    System.out.println(repType);
  }
}
```

With Java 8, you can provide an implementation of a method in
an interface. Java 9 introduces private interface methods.

---

**TIP**

Classes can implement multiple interfaces, and interfaces
can extend multiple interfaces.

---

# Enumerations

In simplest terms, enumerations are a set of objects that represent a related set of choices:

```
enum DisplayButton {ROUND, SQUARE}
DisplayButton round = DisplayButton.ROUND;
```

Looking beyond simplest terms, an enumeration is a class of type enum, and it is a singleton. Enum classes can have methods, constructors, and data members:

```
enum DisplayButton {
    // Size in inches
    ROUND (.50f),
    SQUARE (.40f);
    private final float size;
    DisplayButton(float size) {this.size = size;}
    private float size()  { return size; }
}
```

The method values() returns an array of the ordered list of objects defined for the enum:

```
for (DisplayButton b : DisplayButton.values())
  System.out.println("Button: " + b.size());
```

# Annotation Types

Annotations provide a way to associate metadata (data about data) with program elements at compile time and runtime. Packages, classes, methods, fields, parameters, variables, and constructors can be annotated.

## Built-in Annotations

Java annotations provide a way to obtain metadata about a class. Java has three built-in annotation types, as depicted in Table 5-1. These annotation types are contained in the java.lang package.

Built-in annotations must be placed directly before the item being annotated. They do not throw exceptions. Annotations return primitive types, enumerations, class `String`, class `Class`, annotations, and arrays (of these types).

*Table 5-1. Built-in annotations*

| Annotation type | Description |
| --- | --- |
| @Override | Indicates that the method is intended to override a method in a superclass. |
| @Deprecated | Indicates that a deprecated API is being used or overridden. Java 9 adds forRemoval and since methods. |
| @FunctionalInterface | Defines one and only one abstract method. |
| @SafeVarargs | Coder's assertion that the annotated method or constructor body doesn't perform unsafe operations on its varargs parameter. |
| @SuppressWarnings | Used to selectively suppress warnings. |

The following are examples of annotation use:

```
@Deprecated(forRemoval=true)
  public void method () {
    ;
  }

@Override
  public String toString() {
    return super.toString() + " more";
  }
```

Because `@Override` is a marker annotation, a compile warning will be returned if the method to be overridden cannot be found.

## Developer-Defined Annotations

Developers can define their own annotations using three annotation types. A *marker* annotation has no parameters, a *single value* annotation has a single parameter, and a *multivalue* annotation has multiple parameters.

The definition of an annotation is the symbol @, followed by the word `interface`, followed by the name of the annotation.

Repeated annotations are permitted.

The meta-annotation `Retention` indicates that an annotation should be retained by the VM so that it can be read at runtime. `Retention` is in the package `java.lang.annotation`:

```
@Retention(RetentionPolicy.RUNTIME)
public @interface Feedback {} // Marker
public @interface Feedback {
  String reportName();
} // Single value
public @interface Feedback {
  String reportName();
  String comment() default "None";
} // Multi value
```

Place the user-defined annotation directly before the item being annotated:

```
@Feedback(reportName="Report 1")
public void myMethod() {...}
```

Programs can check the existence of annotations and obtain annotation values by calling `getAnnotation()` on a method:

```
Feedback fb =
  myMethod.getAnnotation(Feedback.class);
```

The Type Annotations Specification (also known as "JSR 308") allows for annotations to be written in array positions and generic type arguments. Annotations may also be written with superclasses, implemented interfaces, casts, `instanceof` checks, exception specifications, wildcards, method references, and constructor references. See *Java SE 8 for the Really Impatient* by Cay S. Horstmann (Addison-Wesley) for detailed information on annotations in these contexts.

# Functional Interfaces

A functional interface, a.k.a. a *single abstract method* (SAM) interface, is an inteface that defines one and only one abstract method. The annotation `@FunctionalInterface` may be placed in front of an interface to declare its intention as a functional interface. It is possible for an interface to have any number of default methods:

```
@FunctionalInterface
  public interface InterfaceName {

  // Only one abstract method allowed
  public void doAbstractTask();

  // Multiple default methods allowed
  default public void performTask1(){
    System.out.println("Msg from task 1.");
  }
  default public void performTask2(){
    System.out.println("Msg from task 2.");
  }
}
```

Instances of functional interfaces can be created with lambda expressions, method references, or constructor references.

# CHAPTER 6

# Statements and Blocks

A statement is a single command that performs some activity when executed by the Java interpreter:

```
GigSim simulator = new GigSim("Let's play gui
tar!");
```

Java statements include the following varieties: expression, empty, block, conditional, iteration, transfer of control, exception handling, variable, labeled, assert, and synchronized.

Reserved Java words used in statements are `if`, `else`, `switch`, `case`, `while`, `do`, `for`, `break`, `continue`, `return`, `synchronized`, `throw`, `try`, `catch`, `finally`, and `assert`.

## Expression Statements

An expression statement is a statement that changes the program state. It is a Java expression that ends in a semicolon. Expression statements include assignments, prefix and postfix increments, prefix and postfix decrements, object creation, and method calls. The following are examples of expression statements:

```
isWithinOperatingHours = true;
++fret; patron++; --glassOfWater; pick--;
```

```
Guitarist guitarist = new Guitarist();
guitarist.placeCapo(guitar, capo, fret);
```

# Empty Statement

The empty statement provides no additional functionality and is written as a single semicolon (;) or as an empty block {}.

# Blocks

A group of statements is called a *block* or *statement block*. A block of statements is enclosed in braces. Variables and classes declared in the block are called *local variables* and *local classes*, respectively. The scope of local variables and classes is the block in which they are declared.

In blocks, one statement is interpreted at a time in the order in which it was written or in the order of flow control. The following is an example of a block:

```
static {
  GigSimProperties.setFirstFestivalActive(true);
  System.out.println("First festival has begun");
  gigsimLogger.info("Simulator started 1st festi
val");
}
```

# Conditional Statements

if, if else, and if else if are decision-making control flow statements. They are used to execute statements conditionally. The expression for any of these statements must have type Boolean or boolean. Type Boolean is subject to unboxing and autoconversion of Boolean to boolean.

## The if Statement

The if statement consists of an expression and a statement or a block of statements that are executed if the expression evaluates to true:

```
Guitar guitar = new Guitar();
guitar.addProblemItem("Whammy bar");
if (guitar.isBroken()) {
  Luthier luthier = new Luthier();
  luthier.repairGuitar(guitar);
}
```

# The if else Statement

When using else with if, the first block of statements is executed if the expression evaluates to true; otherwise, the block of code in the else is executed:

```
CoffeeShop coffeeshop = new CoffeeShop();
if (coffeeshop.getPatronCount() > 5) {
  System.out.println("Play the event.");
} else {
  System.out.println("Go home without pay.");
}
```

# The if else if Statement

if else if is typically used when you need to choose among multiple blocks of code. When the criteria are not met to execute any of the blocks, the block of code in the final else is executed:

```
ArrayList<Song> playList = new ArrayList<>();
Song song1 = new Song("Mister Sandman");
Song song2 = new Song("Amazing Grace");
playList.add(song1);
playList.add(song2);
...
int numOfSongs = playList.size();
if (numOfSongs <= 24) {
  System.out.println("Do not book");
} else if ((numOfSongs > 24) & (numOfSongs < 50)){
  System.out.println("Book for one night");
} else if ((numOfSongs >= 50)) {
  System.out.println("Book for two nights");
} else {
```

```
    System.out.println("Book for the week");
}
```

## The switch Statement

The switch statement is a control flow statement that starts with an expression and transfers control to one of the case statements based on the value of the expression. A switch works with char, byte, short, int, as well as Character, Byte, Short, and Integer wrapper types; enumeration types; and the String type. Support for String objects was added in Java SE 7. The break statement is used to exit out of a switch statement. If a case statement does not contain a break, the line of code after the completion of the case will be executed.

This continues until either a break statement is reached or the end of the switch is reached. One default label is permitted and is often listed last for readability:

```
String style;
String guitarist = "Eric Clapton";
...
switch (guitarist) {
  case "Chet Atkins":
    style = "Nashville sound";
    break;
  case "Thomas Emmanuel":
    style = "Complex fingerstyle";
    break;
  default:
    style = "Unknown";
    break;
}
```

## Iteration Statements

The for loop, enhanced for loop, while, and do-while statements are iteration statements. They are used for iterating through pieces of code.

## The for Loop

The for statement contains three parts: initialization, expression, and update. As shown next, the variable (i.e., i) in the statement must be initialized before being used. The expression (i.e., i<bArray.length) is evaluated before iterating through the loop (i.e., i++). The iteration takes place only if the expression is true and the variable is updated after each iteration:

```
Banjo [] bArray = new Banjo[2];
bArray[0] = new Banjo();
bArray[0].setManufacturer("Windsor");
bArray[1] = new Banjo();
bArray[1].setManufacturer("Gibson");
for (int i=0; i<bArray.length; i++){
   System.out.println(bArray[i].getManufacturer());
}
```

## The Enhanced for Loop

The enhanced for loop, a.k.a. the "for in" loop and "for each" loop, is used for iteration through an iterable object or array. The loop is executed once for each element of the array or collection and does not use a counter, because the number of iterations is already determined:

```
ElectricGuitar eGuitar1 = new ElectricGuitar();
eGuitar1.setName("Blackie");
ElectricGuitar eGuitar2 = new ElectricGuitar();
eGuitar2.setName("Lucille");
ArrayList <ElectricGuitar> eList = new Array
List<>();
eList.add(eGuitar1); eList.add(eGuitar2);
for (ElectricGuitar e : eList) {
   System.out.println("Name:" + e.getName());
}
```

## The while Loop

In a while statement, the expression is evaluated and the loop is executed only if the expression evaluates to true. The expression can be of type boolean or Boolean:

```java
int bandMembers = 5;
while (bandMembers > 3) {
   CoffeeShop c = new CoffeeShop();
   c.performGig(bandMembers);
   // Randomly set zero to seven members
   bandMembers = new Random().nextInt(8);
}
```

## The do while Loop

In a do while statement, the loop is always executed at least once and will continue to be executed as long as the expression is true. The expression can be of type boolean or Boolean:

```java
int bandMembers = 1;
do {
   CoffeeShop c = new CoffeeShop();
   c.performGig(bandMembers);
   Random generator = new Random();
   bandMembers = generator.nextInt(7) + 1; // 1-7
} while (bandMembers > 3);
```

# Transfer of Control

Transfer of control statements are used to change the flow of control in a program. These include the break, continue, and return statements.

## The break Statement

An unlabeled break statement is used to exit the body of a switch statement or to immediately exit the loop in which it is contained. Loop bodies include those for the for loop, enhanced for loop, while, and do-while iteration statements:

```
Song song = new Song("Pink Panther");
Guitar guitar = new Guitar();
int measure = 1; int lastMeasure = 10;
while (measure <= lastMeasure) {
  if (guitar.checkForBrokenStrings()) {
    break;
  }
  song.playMeasure(measure);
  measure++;
}
```

A labeled break forces a break of the loop statement immediately following the label. Labels are typically used with for and while loops when there are nested loops and there is a need to identify which loop to break. To label a loop or a statement, place the label statement immediately before the loop or statement being labeled, as follows:

```
...
playMeasures:
while (isWithinOperatingHours()) {
  while (measure <= lastMeasure) {
    if (guitar.checkForBrokenStrings()) {
      break playMeasures;
    }
    song.playMeasure(measure);
    measure++;
  }
} // exits to here
```

## The continue Statement

When executed, the unlabeled continue statement stops the execution of the current for loop, enhanced for loop, while, or do-while statements and starts the next iteration of the loop. The rules for testing loop conditions apply. A labeled continue statement forces the next iteration of the loop statement immediately following the label:

```
for (int i=0; i<25; i++) {
  if (playList.get(i).isPlayed()) {
```

```
    continue;
  } else {
    song.playAllMeasures();
  }
}
```

## The return Statement

The `return` statement is used to exit a method and return a value if the method specifies a return type:

```
private int numberOfFrets = 18; // default
...
public int getNumberOfFrets() {
  return numberOfFrets;
}
```

The `return` statement will be optional when it is the last statement in a method and the method doesn't return anything.

# Synchronized Statement

The Java keyword `synchronized` can be used to limit access to sections of code (i.e., entire methods) to a single thread. It provides the capability to control access to resources shared by multiple threads. See Chapter 14 for more information.

# Assert Statement

Assertions are Boolean expressions used to check whether code behaves as expected while running in debug mode (i.e., using the `-enableassertions` or `-ea` switch with the Java interpreter). Assertions are written as follows:

```
assert boolean_expression;
```

Assertions help identify bugs more easily, including identifying unexpected values. They are designed to validate assumptions that should always be `true`. While running in debug mode, if the assertion evaluates to `false`, a `java.lang.AssertionError` is thrown and the program exits; otherwise, nothing happens:

```
// 'strings' value should be 4, 5, 6, 7, 8 or 12
assert (strings == 12 ||
  (strings >= 4 && strings <= 8));
```

Assertions need to be explicitly enabled. To find command-line arguments used to enable assertions, see Chapter 10.

Assertions may also be written to include an optional error code. Although called an *error code*, it is really just text or a value to be used for informational purposes only.

When an assertion that contains an error code evaluates to false, the error code value is turned into a string and displayed to the user immediately prior to the program exiting:

```
assert boolean_expression : errorcode;
```

An example of an assertion using an error code is as follows:

```
// Show invalid 'stringed instruments' strings
value
assert (strings == 12 ||
  (strings >= 4 && strings <= 8))
  : "Invalid string count: " + strings;
```

# Exception Handling Statements

Exception handling statements are used to specify code to be executed during unusual circumstances. The keywords throw and try/catch/finally are used for exception handling. For more information on exception handling, see Chapter 7.

# Exception Handling

An *exception* is an anomalous condition that alters or interrupts the flow of execution. Java provides built-in exception handling to deal with such conditions. Exception handling should not be part of the normal program flow.

## The Exception Hierarchy

As shown in Figure 7-1, all exceptions and errors inherit from the class Throwable, which inherits from the class Object.

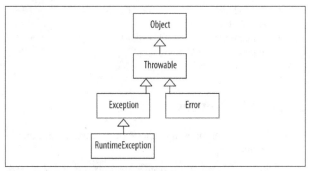

*Figure 7-1. Snapshot of the exception hierarchy*

# Checked/Unchecked Exceptions and Errors

Exceptions and errors fall into three categories: checked exceptions, unchecked exceptions, and errors.

## Checked Exceptions

- Checked exceptions are checked by the compiler at compile time.

- Methods that throw a checked exception must indicate so in the method declaration using the `throws` clause. This must continue all the way up the calling stack until the exception is handled.

- All checked exceptions must be explicitly caught with a `catch` block.

- Checked exceptions include exceptions of the type `Exception`, and all classes that are subtypes of `Exception`, except for `RuntimeException` and the subtypes of `RuntimeException`.

The following is an example of a method that throws a checked exception:

```
// Method declaration that throws
// an IOException
void readFile(String filename)
  throws IOException {
  ...
}
```

## Unchecked Exceptions

- The compiler does not check unchecked exceptions at compile time.

- Unchecked exceptions occur during runtime due to programmer error (e.g., out-of-bounds index, divide by zero, and null pointer exception) or system resource exhaustion.

- Unchecked exceptions do not have to be caught.
- Methods that may throw an unchecked exception do not have to (but can) indicate this in the method declaration.
- Unchecked exceptions include exceptions of the type `RuntimeException` and all subtypes of `RuntimeException`.

## Errors

- Errors are typically unrecoverable and present serious conditions.
- Errors are not checked at compile time and do not have to be (but can be) caught/handled.

---

### TIP

Any checked exceptions, unchecked exceptions, or errors can be caught.

---

# Common Checked/Unchecked Exceptions and Errors

There are various checked exceptions, unchecked exceptions, and unchecked errors that are part of the standard Java platform. Some are more likely to occur than others.

## Common Checked Exceptions

`ClassNotFoundException`
    Thrown when a class cannot be loaded because its definition cannot be found.

IOException
> Thrown when a failed or interrupted operation occurs.
> Two common subtypes of IOException are EOFException
> and FileNotFoundException.

FileNotFoundException
> Thrown when an attempt is made to open a file that can-
> not be found.

SQLException
> Thrown when there is a database error.

InterruptedException
> Thrown when a thread is interrupted.

NoSuchMethodException
> Thrown when a called method cannot be found.

CloneNotSupportedException
> Thrown when clone() is called by an object that is not
> cloneable.

## Common Unchecked Exceptions

ArithmeticException
> Thrown to indicate that an exceptional arithmetic condi-
> tion has occurred.

ArrayIndexOutOfBoundsException
> Thrown to indicate an index is out of range.

ClassCastException
> Thrown to indicate an attempt to cast an object to a sub-
> class of which it is not an instance.

DateTimeException
> Thrown to indicate problems with creating, querying, and
> manipulating date-time objects.

IllegalArgumentException
> Thrown to indicate that an invalid argument has been
> passed to a method.

IllegalStateException
> Thrown to indicate that a method has been called at an inappropriate time.

IndexOutOfBoundsException
> Thrown to indicate that an index is out of range.

NullPointerException
> Thrown when code references a null object but a nonnull object is required.

NumberFormatException
> Thrown to indicate an invalid attempt to convert a string to a numeric type.

UncheckedIOException
> Wraps an IOException with an unchecked exception.

## Common Errors

AssertionError
> Thrown to indicate that an assertion failed.

ExceptionInInitializeError
> Thrown to indicate an unexpected exception in a static initializer.

VirtualMachineError
> Thrown to indicate a problem with the JVM.

OutOfMemoryError
> Thrown when there is no more memory available to allocate an object or perform garbage collection.

NoClassDefFoundError
> Thrown when the JVM cannot find a class definition that was found at compile time.

StackOverflowError
> Thrown to indicate that a stack overflow occurs.

# Exception Handling Keywords

In Java, error-handling code is cleanly separated from error-generating code. Code that generates the exception is said to "throw" an exception, whereas code that handles the exception is said to "catch" the exception:

```
// Declare an exception
public void methodA() throws IOException {
  ...
  throw new IOException();
  ...
}

// Catch an exception
public void methodB() {
  ...
  /* Call to methodA must be in a try/catch block
  ** since the exception is a checked exception;
  ** otherwise methodB could throw the exception */
  try {
      methodA();

  }catch (IOException ioe) {
    System.err.println(ioe.getMessage());
    ioe.printStackTrace();
  }
}
```

## The throw Keyword

To throw an exception, use the keyword throw. Any checked/unchecked exception and error can be thrown:

```
if (n == -1)
  throw new EOFException();
```

## The try/catch/finally Keywords

Thrown exceptions are handled by a Java try, catch, finally block. The Java interpreter looks for code to handle the exception, first looking in the enclosed block of code, and then propagating up the call stack to main() if necessary. If the exception is not handled on the main thread (i.e., not the *Event Dispatch Thread* [EDT]) or a thread that you created, the program exits and a stack trace is printed:

```
try {
  method();
} catch (EOFException eofe) {
  eofe.printStackTrace();
} catch (IOException ioe) {
  ioe.printStackTrace();
} finally {
  // cleanup
}
```

## The try-catch Statement

The try-catch statement includes one try and one or more catch blocks.

The try block contains code that may throw exceptions. All checked exceptions that may be thrown must have a catch block to handle the exception. If no exceptions are thrown, the try block terminates normally. A try block may have zero or more catch clauses to handle the exceptions.

---

### TIP

A try block must have at least one catch or finally block associated with it, or it can omit the catch as long as the method throws the exception.

---

There cannot be any code between the try block and any of the catch blocks (if present) or the finally block (if present).

The catch block(s) contain code to handle thrown exceptions, including printing information about the exception to a file, which gives users an opportunity to input correct information. Note that catch blocks should never be empty because such "silencing" results in exceptions being hidden, which makes errors harder to debug.

A common convention for naming the parameter in the catch clause is a set of letters representing each of the words in the name of the exception:

```
catch (ArrayIndexOutOfBoundsException aioobe) {
  aioobe.printStackStrace();
}
```

Within a catch clause, a new exception may also be thrown if necessary.

The order of the catch clauses in a try/catch block defines the precedence for catching exceptions. Always begin with the most specific exception that may be thrown and end with the most general.

---

### TIP

Exceptions thrown in the try block are directed to the first catch clause containing arguments of the same type as the exception object or superclass of that type. The catch block with the Exception parameter should always be last in the ordered list.

---

If none of the parameters for the catch clauses match the exception thrown, the system will search for the parameter that matches the superclass of the exception.

## The try-finally Statement

The try-finally statement includes one try and one finally block. The finally block is used for releasing resources when necessary:

```java
public void testMethod() throws IOException {
FileWriter fileWriter =
  new FileWriter("\\data.txt");
  try {
    fileWriter.write("Information...");
  } finally {
    fileWriter.close();
  }
}
```

This block is optional and is only used where needed. When used, it is executed last in a try-finally block and will always be executed, whether or not the try block terminates normally. If the finally block throws an exception, it must be handled.

## The try-catch-finally Statement

The try-catch-finally statement includes one try, one or more catch blocks, and one finally block.

For this statement, the finally block is also used for cleanup and releasing resources:

```java
public void testMethod() {
  FileWriter fileWriter = null;
  try {
    fileWriter = new FileWriter("\\data.txt");
    fileWriter.write("Information...");
  } catch (IOException ex) {
    ex.printStackTrace();
  } finally {
    try {
      fileWriter.close();
    } catch (Exception e) {
      e.printStackTrace();
    }
  }
}
```

This block is optional and is only used where needed. When used, it is executed last in a try-catch-finally block and will always be executed, whether or not the try block terminates normally or the catch clause(s) were executed. If the finally block throws an exception, it must be handled.

## The try-with-resources Statement

The try-with-resources statement is used for declaring resources that must be closed when they are no longer needed. These resources are declared in the try block. Java 9 simplifies the statement:

```java
// Java 7 and 8
public void testMethod() throws IOException {
  FileWriter fileWriter = new FileWriter("\
\data.txt");
  try (FileWriter fw = fileWriter)
  {
    fw.write("Information...");
  }
}
// Java 9
public void testMethod() throws IOException {
  FileWriter fileWriter = new FileWriter("\
\data.txt");
  try (fileWriter)
  {
    f1.write("Information...");
  }
}
```

Any resource that implements the AutoClosable interface may be used with the try-with-resources statement.

## The multi-catch Clause

The multi-catch clause is used to allow for multiple exception arguments in one catch clause:

```java
boolean isTest = false;
public void testMethod() {
  try {
```

```
  if (isTest) {
    throw new IOException();
  } else {
    throw new SQLException();
  }
} catch (IOException | SQLException e) {
  e.printStackTrace();
  }
}
```

# The Exception Handling Process

Here are the steps to the exception handling process:

1. An exception is encountered, which results in an exception object being created.

2. A new exception object is thrown.

3. The runtime system looks for code to handle the exception, beginning with the method in which the exception object was created. If no handler is found, the runtime environment traverses the call stack (the ordered list of methods) in reverse looking for an exception handler. If the exception is not handled, the program exits and a stack trace is automatically output.

4. The runtime system hands the exception object off to an exception handler to handle (catch) the exception.

# Defining Your Own Exception Class

Programmer-defined exceptions should be created when those other than the existing Java exceptions are necessary. In general, the Java exceptions should be reused wherever possible:

- To define a checked exception, the new exception class must extend the Exception class, directly or indirectly.

- To define an unchecked exception, the new exception class must extend the `RuntimeException` class, directly or indirectly.

- To define an unchecked error, the new error class must extend the `Error` class.

User-defined exceptions should have at least two constructors —a constructor that does not accept any arguments and a constructor that does:

```
public class ReportException extends Exception {
  public ReportException () {}
  public ReportException (String message, int
    reportId) {
    ...
  }
}
```

If catching an exception and throwing a more specific exception, it is wise to always capture the base exception.

# Printing Information About Exceptions

The methods in the `Throwable` class that provide information about thrown exceptions are `getMessage()`, `toString`, and `printStackTrace()`. In general, one of these methods should be called in the `catch` clause handling the exception. Programmers can also write code to obtain additional useful information when an exception occurs (i.e., the name of the file that was not found).

## The getMessage() Method

The `getMessage()` method returns a detailed message string about the exception:

```
try {
  new FileReader("file.js");
} catch (FileNotFoundException fnfe) {
```

```
  System.err.println(fnfe.getMessage());
}
```

## The toString() Method

This toString() method returns a detailed message string about the exception, including its class name:

```
try {
  new FileReader("file.js");
} catch (FileNotFoundException fnfe) {
    System.err.println(fnfe.toString());
}
```

## The printStackTrace() Method

This printStackTrace() method returns a detailed message string about the exception, including its class name and a stack trace from where the error was caught, all the way back to where it was thrown:

```
try {
  new FileReader("file.js");
} catch (FileNotFoundException fnfe) {
  fnfe.printStackTrace();
}
```

The following is an example of a stack trace. The first line contains the contents returned when the toString() method is invoked on an exception object. The remainder shows the method calls, beginning with the location where the exception was thrown and going all the way back to where it was caught and handled:

```
java.io.FileNotFoundException: file.js (The system
cannot find the file specified)
 at java.io.FileInputStream.open(Native Method)
 at java.io.FileInputStream.(init)
 (FileInputSteam.java:106)
 at java.io.FileInputStream.(init)
 (FileInputSteam.java:66)
 at java.io.FileReader(init)(FileReader.java:41)
```

```
at EHExample.openFile(EHExample.java:24)
at EHExample.main(EHExample.java:15)
```

---

### TIP

Java 9 introduces a Stack-Walking API that allows easy filtering of and lazy access to the information in stack traces.

---

# CHAPTER 8

# Java Modifiers

Modifiers, which are Java keywords, may be applied to classes, interfaces, constructors, methods, and data members.

Table 8-1 lists the Java modifiers and their applicability. Note that private and protected classes are allowed, but only as inner or nested classes. Reference Chapter 21 for accessibility details relative to Java 9.

*Table 8-1. Java modifiers*

| Modifier | Class | Interface | Constructor | Method | Data member |
|---|---|---|---|---|---|
| *Access modifiers* | | | | | |
| *package-private* | Yes | Yes | Yes | Yes | Yes |
| private | No | No | Yes | Yes | Yes |
| protected | No | No | Yes | Yes | Yes |
| public | Yes | Yes | Yes | Yes | Yes |
| *Other modifiers* | | | | | |
| abstract | Yes | Yes | No | Yes | No |
| final | Yes | No | No | Yes | Yes |
| native | No | No | No | Yes | No |
| strictfp | Yes | Yes | No | Yes | No |

| Modifier | Class | Interface | Constructor | Method | Data member |
|---|---|---|---|---|---|
| `static` | No | No | No | Yes | Yes |
| `synchronized` | No | No | No | Yes | No |
| `transient` | No | No | No | No | Yes |
| `volatile` | No | No | No | No | Yes |

Inner classes may also use the `private` or `protected` access modifiers. Local variables may only use one modifier: `final`.

## Access Modifiers

Access modifiers define the access privileges of classes, interfaces, constructors, methods, and data members. Access modifiers consist of `public`, `private`, and `protected`. If no modifier is present, the default access of *package-private* is used.

Table 8-2 provides details on visibility when access modifiers are used.

*Table 8-2. Access modifiers and their visibility*

| Modifier | Visibility |
|---|---|
| *package-private* | The default *package-private* limits access from within the package. |
| `private` | The `private` method is accessible from within its class. The `private` data member is accessible from within its class or interface (Java 9). It can be indirectly accessed through methods (i.e., getter and setter methods). |
| `protected` | The `protected` method is accessible from within its package, and also from outside its package by subclasses of the class containing the method. The `protected` data member is accessible within its package, and also from outside its package by subclasses of the class containing the data member. |

| Modifier | Visibility |
|---|---|
| public | The public modifier allows access from anywhere, even outside of the package in which it was declared. Note that interfaces are public by default. |

# Other (Nonaccess) Modifiers

Table 8-3 contains the nonaccess Java modifiers and their usage.

*Table 8-3. Nonaccess Java modifiers*

| Modifier | Usage |
|---|---|
| abstract | An abstract class is a class that is declared with the keyword abstract. It cannot be simultaneously declared with final. Interfaces are abstract by default and do not have to be declared abstract.<br>An abstract method is a method that contains only a signature and no body. If at least one method in a class is abstract, then the enclosing class is abstract. It cannot be declared final, native, private, static, or synchronized. |
| default | A default method, a.k.a. defender method, allows for the creation of a default method implementation in an interface. |
| final | A final class cannot be extended.<br>A final method cannot be overridden.<br>A final data member is initialized only once and cannot be changed. A data member that is declared static final is set at compile time and cannot be changed. |
| native | A native method is used to merge other programming languages such as C and C++ code into a Java program. It contains only a signature and no body. It cannot be used simultaneously with strictfp. |

| Modifier | Usage |
|---|---|
| static | Both static methods and static variables are accessed through the class name. They are used for the whole class and all instantiations from that class.<br>A static data member is accessed through the class name. Only one static data member exists, no matter how many instances of the class exist. |
| strictfp | A strictfp class will follow the IEEE 754-1985 floating-point specification for all of its floating-point operations.<br>A strictfp method has all expressions in the method as FP-strict. Methods within interfaces cannot be declared strictfp. It cannot be used simultaneously with the native modifier. |
| synchronized | A synchronized method allows only one thread to execute the method block at a time, making it thread safe. Statements can also be synchronized. |
| transient | A transient data member is not serialized when the class is serialized. It is not part of the persistent state of an object. |
| volatile | A volatile data member informs a thread, both to get the latest value for the variable (instead of using a cached copy) and to write all updates to the variable as they occur. |

## Modifiers Encoding

Modifiers applied to classes and members can be retrieved with
Class.getModifiers() and Member.getModifiers(), respectively. The modifiers are encoded, and can be decoded with
Modifier.toString(value):

```
// Modifiers used on the HashMap class
Class c = new HashMap().getClass();
String modifiers = Modifier.toString(c.getModifi
ers());
System.out.println("Class Modifier(s) = " + modi
fiers);
$ Class Modifier(s) = public

// Modifiers used on the Hashmap isEmpty
```

```
// member/method
Member m = new HashMap().getClass().getDeclaredMe
thod("isEmpty");
String modifiers = Modifier.toString(m.getModifi
ers());
System.out.println("Method Modifier(s) = " + modi
fiers);
$ Method Modifier(s) = public
```

# PART II
# Platform

# CHAPTER 9

# Java Platform, Standard Edition

The Java Platform, Standard Edition (SE), includes the *Java Runtime Environment* (JRE) and its encompassing *Java Development Kit* (JDK; see Chapter 10), the Java Programming Language, *Java Virtual Machines* (JVMs), tools/utilities, and the Java SE API libraries. A variety of platforms are available including Windows, macOS, Linux, and Solaris.

## Common Java SE API Libraries

Java SE 9 API standard libraries (*http://download.java.net/java/jdk9/docs/api/*) are provided within packages (and modules). Each package is made up of classes and/or interfaces. An abbreviated list of commonly used packages is represented here to demonstrate the capabilities of the API. They are listed outside of the module ordering in JDK 9.

Java SE provides the JavaFX runtime libraries from Java SE 7 update 6 and JavaFX 2.2 onwards (*http://bit.ly/1gvdiNC*). JavaFX has replaced the Swing API as the primary client UI library for Java SE.

## Language and Utility Libraries

java.lang

> Language support: system/math methods, fundamental types, strings, threads, and exceptions

java.lang.annotation

> Annotation framework: metadata library support

java.lang.instrument

> Program instrumentation: agent services to instrument JVM programs

java.lang.invoke

> Dynamic Language Support: supported by core classes and VM

java.lang.management

> Java Management Extensions API: JVM monitoring and management

java.lang.module

> Module descriptors and configurations support

java.lang.ref

> Reference-object classes: interaction support with the GC

java.lang.reflect

> Reflective information about classes and objects

java.util

> Utilities: collections, event model, date/time, and international support

java.util.concurrent

> Concurrency utilities: executors, queues, timing, and synchronizers

java.util.concurrent.atomic

> Atomic toolkit: lock-free thread-safe programming on single variables

java.util.concurrent.locks

> Locking framework: locks and conditions

`java.util.function`
> Functional interfaces: provides target types for lambda expressions and method references

`java.util.jar`
> Java Archive file format: reading and writing

`java.util.logging`
> Logging: failures, errors, performance issues, and bugs

`java.util.prefs`
> User and system preferences: retrieval and storage

`java.util.regex`
> Regular expressions: char sequences matched to patterns

`java.util.stream`
> Streams: functional-style operations on streams of elements

`java.util.zip`
> ZIP and GZIP file formats: reading and writing

## Base Libraries

`java.beans`
> Beans: components based on JavaBeans, long-term persistence

`java.beans.beancontext`
> Bean context: containers for beans, run environments

`java.io`
> Input/output: through data streams, the filesystem, and serialization

`java.math`
> Mathematics: extra large integer and decimal arithmetic

`java.net`
> Networking: TCP, UDP, sockets, and addresses

`java.nio`
> High performance I/O: buffers, memory-mapped files

`java.nio.channels`
Channels for I/O: selectors for nonblocking I/O

`java.nio.charset`
Character sets: translation between bytes and Unicode

`java.nio.file`
File support: files, file attributes, filesystems

`java.nio.file.attribute`
File and filesystem attribute support

`java.text`
Text utilities: text, dates, numbers, and messages

`java.time`
Time: dates, times, instants, and durations

`java.time.chrono`
Time: calendar systems

`java.time.format`
Time: printing and parsing

`java.time.temporal`
Time: access using fields, units, and adjusters

`java.time.zone`
Time: support for time zones and their rules

`javax.annotation`
Annotation types: library support

`javax.management`
JMX API: application configuration, statistics, and state changes

`javax.net`
Networking: socket factories

`javax.net.http`
High level HTTP and WebSocket API

`javax.net.ssl`

Secured sockets layer: error detection, data encryption/authentication

`javax.tools`

Program invoked tool interfaces: compilers, file managers

## Integration Libraries

`java.sql`

*Structured Query Language* (SQL): access and processing data source information

`javax.jws`

Java web services: supporting annotation types

`javax.jws.soap`

Java web services: SOAP bindings and message parameters

`javax.naming`

Naming services: *Java Naming and Directory Interface* (JNDI)

`javax.naming.directory`

Directory services: JNDI operations for directory-stored objects

`javax.naming.event`

Event services: JNDI event notification operations

`javax.naming.ldap`

Lightweight Directory Access Protocol v3: operations and controls

`javax.script`

Scripting language support: integration, bindings, and invocations

`javax.sql`

SQL: database APIs and server-side capabilities

`javax.sql.rowset.serial`

Serializable mappings: between SQL types and data types

`javax.sql.rowset`
Java Database Connectivity (JDBC) Rowset: standard interfaces

`javax.transactions.xa`
XA Interface: transaction and resource manager contracts for JTA

## Miscellaneous User Interface Libraries

`javax.accessibility`
Accessibility technology: assistive support for UI components

`javax.imageio`
Java image I/O: image file content description (metadata, thumbnails)

`javax.print`
Print services: formatting and job submissions

`javax.print.attribute`
Java Print Services: attributes and attribute set collecting

`javax.print.attribute.standard`
Standard attributes: widely used attributes and values

`javax.print.event`
Printing events: services and print job monitoring

`javax.sound.midi`
Sound: I/O, sequencing, and synthesis of MIDI Types 0 and 1

`javax.sound.sampled`
Sound: sampled audio data (AIFF, AU, and WAV formats)

## JavaFX User Interface Library

`javafx.animation`
Transition-based animation

`javafx.application`
Application life cycle

`javafx.beans`
Generic form of observability

`javafx.beans.binding`
Binding characteristics

`javafx.beans.property`
Read-only and writable properties

`javafx.beans.property.adapter`
Property adapter

`javafx.beans.value`
Reading and writing

`javafx.collections`
JavaFX collection utilities

`javafx.concurrent`
JavaFX concurrent task

`javafx.embed.swing`
Swing API application integration

`javafx.embed.swt`
SWT API application integration

`javafx.event`
Event framework (e.g., delivery and handling)

`javafx.fxml`
Markup language (e.g., loading an object hierarchy)

`javafx.geometry`
Two-dimensional geometry

`javafx.scene`
Base classes: core Scene Graph API

`javafx.scene.canvas`
Canvas classes: an immediate mode style of rendering API

`javafx.scene.chart`
Chart components: data visualization

`javafx.scene.control`
User interface controls: specialized nodes in the scene graph

`javafx.scene.control.cell`
Cell-related classes (i.e., noncore classes)

`javafx.scene.effect`
Graphical filter effects: supporting scene graph nodes

`javafx.scene.image`
Loading and displaying images

`javafx.scene.input`
Mouse and keyboard input event handling

`javafx.scene.layout`
Interface layout classes

`javafx.scene.media`
Audio and video classes

`javafx.scene.paint`
Colors and gradients support (e.g., fill shapes and backgrounds)

`javafx.scene.shape`
Two-dimensional shapes

`javafx.scene.text`
Fonts and text node rendering

`javafx.scene.transform`
Transformation: rotating, scaling, shearing, and translation for affine objects

`javafx.scene.web`
Web content: loading and displaying web content

`javafx.stage`
Stage: top-level container

```
javafx.util
```
Utilities and helper classes

```
javafx.util.converter
```
String converters

# Remote Method Invocation (RMI) and CORBA Libraries

```
java.rmi
```
Remote Method Invocation: invokes objects on remote JVMs

```
java.rmi.activation
```
RMI object activation: activates persistent remote object's references

```
java.rmi.dgc
```
RMI distributed garbage collection (DGC): remote object tracking from client

```
java.rmi.registry
```
RMI registry: remote object that maps names to remote objects

```
java.rmi.server
```
RMI server side: RMI transport protocol, Hypertext Transfer Protocol (HTTP) tunneling, stubs

```
javax.rmi
```
Remote Method Invocation (RMI): Remote Method Invocation Internet InterORB Protocol (RMI-IIOP), Java Remote Method Protocol (JRMP), Java Remote Method Protocol (JRMP)

```
javax.rmi.CORBA
```
Common Object Request Broker Architecture (CORBA) support: portability APIs for RMI-IIOP and Object Request Brokers (ORBs)

`javax.rmi.ssl`

Secured Sockets Layer (SSL): RMI client and server support

`org.omg.CORBA`

OMG CORBA: CORBA to Java mapping, ORBs

`org.omg.CORBA_2_3`

OMG CORBA additions: further Java Compatibility Kit (JCK) test support

## Security Libraries

`java.security`

Security: algorithms, mechanisms, and protocols

`java.security.cert`

Certifications: parsing, managing Certificate Revocation Lists (CRLs) and certification paths

`java.security.interfaces`

Security interfaces: Rivest, Shamir, and Adelman (RSA) and Digital Signature Algorithm (DSA) generation

`java.security.spec`

Specifications: security keys and algorithm parameters

`javax.crypto`

Cryptographic operations: encryption, keys, MAC generations

`javax.crypto.interfaces`

Diffie-Hellman keys: defined in RSA Laboratories' PKCS #3

`javax.crypto.spec`

Specifications: for security key and algorithm parameters

`javax.security.auth`

Security authentication and authorization: access controls specifications `javax.security.auth.callback`

Authentication callback support: services interaction with apps

`javax.security.auth.kerberos`

Kerberos network authentication protocol: related utility classes

`javax.security.auth.login`

Login and configuration: pluggable authentication framework

`javax.security.auth.x500`

X500 Principal and X500 Private Credentials: subject storage

`javax.security.sasl`

Simple Authentication and Security Layer (SASL): SASL authentication

`org.ietf.jgss`

Java Generic Security Service (JGSS): authentication, data integrity

## Extensible Markup Language (XML) Libraries

`javax.xml`

Extensible Markup Language (XML): constants

`javax.xml.bind`

XML runtime bindings: unmarshalling, marshalling, and validation

`javax.xml.catalog`

XML catalog support: XML Catalogs OASIS Standard V1.1, 7 October 2005

`javax.xml.crypto`

XML cryptography: signature generation and data encryption

`javax.xml.crypto.dom`
> XML and Document Object Model (DOM): cryptographic implementations

`javax.xml.crypto.dsig`
> XML digital signatures: generating and validating

`javax.xml.datatype`
> XML and Java data types: mappings

`javax.xml.namespace`
> XML namespaces: processing

`javax.xml.parsers`
> XML parsers: Simple API for XML (SAX) and DOM parsers

`javax.xml.soap`
> XML; SOAP messages: creation and building

`javax.xml.transform`
> XML transformation processing: no DOM or SAX dependency

`javax.xml.transform.dom`
> XML transformation processing: DOM-specific API

`javax.xml.transform.sax`
> XML transformation processing: SAX-specific API

`javax.xml.transform.stax`
> XML transformation processing: Streaming API for XML (StAX) API

`javax.xml.validation`
> XML validation: verification against XML schema

`javax.xml.ws`
> Java API for XML Web Services (JAX-WS): core APIs

`javax.xml.ws.handler`
> JAX-WS message handlers: message context and handler interfaces

`javax.xml.ws.handler.soap`
    JAX-WS: SOAP message handlers

`javax.xml.ws.http`
    JAX-WS: HTTP bindings

`javax.xml.ws.soap`
    JAX-WS: SOAP bindings

`javax.xml.xpath`
    XPath expressions: evaluation and access

`org.w3c.dom`
    W3C's DOM: file content and structure access and updates

`org.xml.sax`
    XML.org's SAX: file content and structure access and updates

# CHAPTER 10

# Development Basics

The Java Runtime Environment (JRE) provides the backbone for running Java applications. The Java Development Kit (JDK) provides all of the components and necessary resources to develop Java applications.

## Java Runtime Environment

The JRE is a collection of software that allows a computer system to run a Java application. The software collection consists of the Java Virtual Machines (JVMs) that interpret Java bytecode into machine code, standard class libraries, user interface toolkits, and a variety of utilities.

## Java Development Kit

The JDK is a programming environment for compiling, debugging, and running Java applications and Java Beans. The JDK includes the JRE with the addition of the Java programming language and additional development tools and tool APIs. Oracle's JDK supports macOS, Solaris, Linux (Oracle, Suse, Red Hat, Ubuntu, and Debian [on ARM]), and Microsoft Windows (Server 2008 R2, Server 2012, Vista, Windows 7, Windows 8, and Windows 10). Additional operating-system and special-purpose JVMs, JDKs, and JREs are freely available from Java Virtual Machine (*http://bit.ly/16mhI6k*).

Table 10-1 lists versions of the JDK provided by Oracle. Download the most recent version at Oracle's website (*http://bit.ly/16mhImY*), where you can also download older versions (*http://bit.ly/16mhHzq*).

*Table 10-1. Java Development Kits*

| Java Development Kits | Codename | Release | Packages | Classes |
|---|---|---|---|---|
| Java SE 9 with JDK 1.9.0 | --- | 2017 | ~225 | ~4,413 |
| Java SE 8 with JDK 1.8.0 | --- | 2014 | 217 | 4,240 |
| Java SE 7 with JDK 1.7.0 | Dolphin | 2011 | 209 | 4,024 |
| Java SE 6 with JDK 1.6.0 | Mustang | 2006 | 203 | 3,793 |
| Java 2 SE 5.0 with JDK 1.5.0 | Tiger | 2004 | 166 | 3,279 |
| Java 2 SE with SDK 1.4.0 | Merlin | 2002 | 135 | 2,991 |
| Java 2 SE with SDK 1.3 | Kestrel | 2000 | 76 | 1,842 |
| Java 2 with SDK 1.2 | Playground | 1998 | 59 | 1,520 |
| Development Kit 1.1 | --- | 1997 | 23 | 504 |
| Development Kit 1.0 | Oak | 1996 | 8 | 212 |

Java SE version 7 reached Oracle's End of Public Updates in April 2015.

# Java Program Structure

Java source files are created with text editors such as jEdit, TextPad, Vim, Notepad++, or one provided by a Java Integrated Development Environment (IDE). The source files must have the *.java* extension and the same name as the public class name contained in the file. If the class has *package-private* access, the class name can differ from the filename.

Therefore, a source file named *HelloWorld.java* would correspond to the public class named HelloWorld, as represented in the following example (all nomenclature in Java is case-sensitive):

```
1 package com.oreilly.tutorial;
2 import java.time.*;
3 // import java.time.ZoneId;;
4 // import java.time.Clock;
5
6 public class HelloWorld
7 {
8   public static void main(String[] args)
9   {
10    ZoneId zi = ZoneId.systemDefault();
11    Clock c = Clock.system(zi);
12    System.out.print("From: "
13      + c.getZone().getId());
13    System.out.println(", \"Hello, World!\"");
14  }
15 }
```

In line 1, the class HelloWorld is contained in the package com.oreilly.tutorial. This package name implies that *com/oreilly/tutorial* is a directory structure that is accessible on the class path for the compiler and the runtime environment. Packaging source files is optional but recommended to avoid conflicts with other software packages.

In line 2, the import declaration allows the JVM to search for classes from other packages. Here, the asterisk makes all classes in the java.time package available. However, you should always explicitly include classes so that dependencies are documented, including the statements import java.time. ZoneId; and import java.time.Clock;, which as you see are currently commented out and would have been a better choice than simply using import java.time.\*;. Note that import statements are not needed because you can include the full package name before each class name; however, this is not an ideal way to code.

In line 6, there must be only one top-level `public` class defined
in a source file. In addition, the file may include multiple top-
level *package-private* classes.

Looking at line 8, we note that Java applications must have a
`main` method. This method is the entry point into a Java program, and it must be defined. The modifiers must be declared
`public`, `static`, and `void`. The arguments parameter provides a
string array of command-line arguments.

In lines 12 and 13, the statements provide calls to the `Sys
tem.out.print` and `System.out.println` methods to print out
the supplied text to the console window.

# Command-Line Tools

A JDK provides several command-line tools that aid in software development. Commonly used tools include the compiler,
launcher/interpreter, archiver, and documenter. Find a complete list of tools at Oracle.com (*http://bit.ly/16mhHQ3*).

## Java Compiler

The Java compiler translates Java source files into Java bytecode. The compiler creates a bytecode file with the same name

as the source file but with the *.class* extension. Here is a list of commonly used compiler options:

`javac [-options] [source files]`
Compiles Java source files.

`javac HelloWorld.java`
Compiles the program to produce *HelloWorld.class*.

`javac -cp /dir/Classes/ HelloWorld.java`
The -cp and -classpath options are equivalent and identify classpath directories to utilize at compile time.

`javac -d /opt/hwapp/classes HelloWorld.java`
The -d option places generated class files into a preexisting, specified directory. If there is a package definition, the path will be included (e.g., */opt/hwapp/classes/com/oreilly/tutorial/*).

`javac -s /opt/hwapp/src HelloWorld.java`
The -s option places generated source files into a preexisting, specified directory. If there is a package definition, the path will be further expanded (e.g., */opt/hwapp/src/com/oreilly/tutorial/*).

`javac --release 8 HelloWorld.java`
The -release option compiles for a specific VM version, supporting Java 6, 7, 8, and 9.

`javac -source 1.8 HelloWorld.java`
The -source option provides source compatibility with the given release, allowing unsupported keywords to be used as identifiers.

`javac -X`
The -X option prints a synopsis of nonstandard options. For example, -Xlint:unchecked enables recommended warnings, which prints out further details for unchecked or unsafe operations.

Even though -Xlint and other -X options are commonly found among Java compilers, the -X options are not standardized, so their availability across JDKs should not be assumed.

```
javac -version
```
The -version option prints the version of the *javac* utility.

```
javac -help
```
The -help option, or the absence of arguments, will cause the help information for the *javac* command to be printed.

See Chapter 21 to see how *javac* has been extended with additional parameters for handling modules.

## Java Interpreter

The Java interpreter handles the program execution, including launching the application. Here is a list of commonly used interpreter options:

```
java [-options] class [arguments...]
```
Runs the interpreter.

```
java [-options] -jar jarfile [arguments...]
```
Executes a JAR file.

```
java HelloWorld
```
Starts the JRE, loads the class HelloWorld, and runs the main method of the class.

```
java com.oreilly.tutorial.HelloWorld
```
Starts the JRE, loads the HelloWorld class under the *com/oreilly/tutorial/* directory, and runs the main method of the class.

```
java [-cp | -classpath] /tmp/Classes HelloWorld
```
The -cp and –classpath options identify classpath directories to use at runtime.

```
java -Dsun.java2d.ddscale=true HelloWorld
```
The -D option sets a system property value. Here, hardware accelerator scaling is turned on.

```
java [-ea | enableassertions] HelloWorld
```
The -ea and –enableassertions options enable Java assertions. Assertions are diagnostic code that you insert in your application. For more information on assertions, see "Assert Statement" on page 70.

```
java [-da | disableassertions] HelloWorld
```
The -da and -disableassertions options disable Java assertions.

```
java –client HelloWorld
```
The -client option selects the client virtual machine to enhance interactive applications such as GUIs.

```
java –server HelloWorld
```
The -server option selects the server virtual machine to enhance overall system performance.

```
java -splash:images/world.gif HelloWorld
```
The -splash option accepts an argument to display a splash screen of an image prior to running the application.

```
java –version
```
The -version option prints the version of the Java interpreter, the JRE, and the virtual machine.

```
java -help
```
The -help option, or the absence of arguments, will cause the help information for the java command to be printed.

```
javaw <classname>
```
On the Windows OS, javaw is equivalent to the java command but without a console window. The Linux equivalent is accomplished by running the java command as a

background process with the ampersand: `java <class name> &`.

## Java Program Packager

The *Java Archive* (JAR) utility is an archiving and compression tool, typically used to combine multiple files into a single file called a *JAR file*. JAR consists of a ZIP archive containing a manifest file (JAR content describer) and optional signature files (for security). Here is a list of commonly used JAR options, along with examples:

```
jar [options] [jar-file] [manifest-files] [entry-point]
[-C dir] files…
```
This is the usage for the JAR utility.

```
jar cf files.jar HelloWorld.java com/oreilly/tutorial/
HelloWorld.class
```
The c option allows for the creation of a JAR file. The f option allows for the specification of the filename. In this example, *HelloWorld.java* and *com/oreilly/tutorial/HelloWorld.class* are included in the JAR file.

```
jar tfv files.jar
```
The t option is used to list the table of contents of the JAR file. The f option is used to specify the filename. The v option lists the contents in verbose format.

```
jar xf files.jar
```
The x option allows for the extraction of the contents of the JAR file. The f option allows for the specification of the filename.

---

### TIP

Several other ZIP tools (e.g., 7-Zip, WinZip, and Win-RAR) can work with JAR files.

---

## JAR File Execution

JAR files can be created so that they are executable by specifying the file within the JAR where the "main" class resides, so the Java interpreter knows which main() method to utilize. Here is a complete example of making a JAR file executable:

1. Create a *HelloWorld.java* file from the HelloWorld class at the beginning of this chapter.

2. Create the subfolders *com/oreilly/tutorial/*.

3. Run javac HelloWorld.

   Use this command to compile the program and place the *HelloWorld.class* file into the *com/oreilly/tutorial/* directory.

4. Create a file named *Manifest.txt* in the directory where the package is located. In the file, include the following line specifying where the main class is located:

   ```
   Main-Class: com.oreilly.tutorial.HelloWorld
   ```

5. Execute jar cmf Manifest.txt helloWorld.jar com/oreilly/tutorial.

   Use this command to create a JAR file that adds the *Manifest.txt* contents to the manifest file, *MANIFEST.MF*. The manifest file is also used to define extensions and various package-related data:

   ```
   Manifest-Version: 1.0
   Created-By: 1.7.0 (Oracle Corporation)
   Main-Class: com.oreilly.tutorial.HelloWorld
   ```

6. Run jar tf HelloWorld.jar.

   Use this command to display the contents of the JAR file:

   ```
   META-INF/
   META-INF/MANIFEST.MF
   com/
   com/oreilly/
   com/oreilly/tutorial
   com/oreilly/tutorial/HelloWorld.class
   ```

7. Finally, run `java -jar HelloWorld.jar`.

Use this command to execute the JAR file.

# Classpath

The classpath (i.e., primary focus through Java 8) is an argument set used by several command-line tools that tells the JVM where to look for user-defined classes and packages. Classpath conventions differ among operating systems.

On Microsoft Windows, directories within paths are delineated with backslashes, and the semicolon is used to separate the paths:

```
-classpath \home\XClasses\;dir\YClasses\;.
```

On POSIX-compliant operations systems (e.g., Solaris, Linux, and macOS), directories within paths are delineated with forward slashes, and a colon is used to separate the paths:

```
-classpath /home/XClasses/:dir/YClasses/:.
```

---

**TIP**

The period represents the current working directory.

---

The CLASSPATH environmental variable can also be set to tell the Java compiler where to look for class files and packages:

```
rem Windows
set CLASSPATH=classpath1;classpath2

# Linux, Solaris, macOS
# (May vary due to shell specifics)
setenv CLASSPATH classpath1:classpath2
```

# CHAPTER 11

# Memory Management

Java has automatic memory management, which is also known as *garbage collection* (GC). GC's principal tasks are allocating memory, maintaining referenced objects in memory, and recovering memory from objects that no longer have references to them.

## Garbage Collectors

Since the J2SE 5.0 release, the Java HotSpot Virtual Machine performs self-tuning. This process includes the attempted best-fit GC and related settings at startup, based on platform information, as well as ongoing GC tuning.

Although the initial settings and runtime tuning for GC are generally successful, there are times when you may wish to change or tune your GC based on the following goals:

*Maximum pause time goal*
> The maximum pause time goal is the desired time that the GC pauses the application to recover memory.

*Throughput goal*
> The throughput goal is the desired application time, or the time spent outside of GC.

The following sections provide an overview of various garbage collectors, their main focus, and situations in which they should be used. "Command-Line Options" on page 122 explains how to acquire information for manually selecting the GC.

## Serial Collector

The serial collector is performed via a single thread on a single CPU. When this GC thread is run, the execution of the application will pause until the collection is complete.

This collection is best used when your application has a small data set, up to approximately 100 MB, and does not have a requirement for low pause times.

## Parallel Collector

The parallel collector, also known as the *throughput collector*, can be performed with multiple threads across several CPUs. Using these multiple threads significantly speeds up GC.

This collector is best used when there are no pause time constraints and application performance is the most important aspect of your program.

## Parallel Compacting Collector

The parallel compacting collector is similar to the parallel collector, except for refined algorithms that reduce collection pause times.

This collector is best used for applications that do have pause time constraints.

---

### TIP

The parallel compacting collector is available beginning with J2SE 5.0 update 6.

---

## Concurrent Mark-Sweep Collector

The Concurrent Mark-Sweep (CMS), also known as the *low-latency collector*, implements algorithms to handle large collections that might warrant long pauses.

This collector is best used when response times take precedence over throughput times and GC pauses.

## Garbage-First (G1) Collector

The Garbage-First collector, also known as the *G1 collector*, is used for multiprocessor machines with large memories. This server-style GC meets pause time goals with high probability, while achieving high throughput. Whole-heap operations (e.g., global marking) are performed concurrently with the application threads, which prevents interruptions proportional to the heap or live-data size.

---

#### TIP

Java SE 9 has made G1 the default garbage collector on 32-bit and 64-bit server configurations. G1 has been available since Java SE 7 update 4

---

# Memory Management Tools

Although tuning your GC may prove to be successful, it is important to note that the GCs do not provide guarantees, only goals; however, any improvement gained on one platform may be undone on another. It is best to find the source of the problem with memory management tools, including profilers.

Table 11-1 lists such tools. All are command-line applications, except Heap/CPU Profiling Tool (HPROF). HPROF is dynamically loaded from a command-line option.

*Table 11-1. JDK memory management tools*

| Resource | Description |
|----------|-------------|
| jvisualvm | Troubleshooting tool packaged in Java 8 but external to 9 |
| jconsole | Java Management Extensions (JMX)-compliant monitoring tool |
| jinfo | Configuration information tool |
| jstat | JVM statistics monitoring tool |
| jstatd | jstat with remote tools attachment |
| jmc | Profiling, monitoring, and diagnostics tools |
| jmap | Memory map tool |
| jstack | Stack trace tool |
| jcmd | Diagnostic command request tool |
| jdb | Java debugger tool |
| jps | Instrumented JVMs listing tool |

---

#### TIP

Consider exploring Oracle Java SE Advanced, which includes Java Mission Control (i.e., jmc) and Java Flight Recorder. These are enterprise-grade, production-savvy diagnostics and monitoring tools. Java Flight Recorder requires a commercial license for use in production.

---

## Command-Line Options

The following GC-related command-line options can be passed into the Java interpreter to interface with the functionality of the Java HotSpot Virtual Machine:

`-XX:+PrintGC` *or* `-verbose:gc`

Prints out general information about the heap and garbage collection at each collection. GC logging uses the unified JVM logging framework as of Java 9.

---

`-XX:+PrintCommandLineFlags -version`

Prints out heap settings, applied -XX values, and version information.

`-XX:+PrintGCDetails`

Prints out detailed information about the heap and garbage collection during each collection.

`-XX:+PrintGCTimeStamps`

Adds timestamps to the output from `PrintGC` or `PrintGCDetails`.

`-XX:+UseSerialGC`

Enables the serial collector.

`-XX:+UseParallelGC`

Enables the parallel collector for scavenges.

`-XX:+UseParallelOldGC`

Enables the parallel collector for full collectors.

`-XX:+UseParNewGC`

Enables the parallel young generation collector. Can be used with the concurrent low pause collector. Removed in Java 9.

`-XX:+UseConcMarkSweepGC`

Enables the concurrent low pause CMS collector. Can be used with the parallel young generation collector. Removed in Java 9.

`-XX:+UseG1GC`

Enables the Garbage-First collector.

`-XX:+DisableExplicitGC`

Disables the explicit GC (`System.gc()`) methods.

`-XX:ParallelGCThreads=[`*threads*`]`

Defines the number of GC threads. The default correlates to the number of CPUs. This option applies to the CMS and parallel collectors.

`-XX:MaxGCPauseMillis=[milliseconds]`

Provides a hint to the GC for the desired maximum pause time goal in milliseconds. This option applies to the parallel collectors.

`-XX:+GCTimeRatio=[__value__]`

Provides a hint to the GC for the desired ratio of GC time to application time $(1 / (1 + [value]))$ for the desired throughput goal. The default value is 99. This means that the application will run 99% of the time, and therefore the GC will run 1% of the time. This option applies to the parallel collectors.

`-XX:+CMSIncrementalMode`

Enables incremental mode for the CMS collector only. Used for machines with one or two processors. Removed in Java 9.

`-XX:+CMSIncrementalPacing`

Enables automatic packing for the CMS collector only.

`-XX:MinHeapFreeRatio=[percent]`

Sets the minimum target percent for the proportion of free space to total heap size. The default percent is 40.

`-XX:MaxHeapFreeRatio=[percent]`

Sets the maximum target percent for the proportion of free space to total heap size. The default percent is 70.

`-Xms[bytes]`

Overrides the minimum heap size in bytes. Default: 1/64 of the system's physical memory up to 1 GB. Initial heap size is 4 MB for machines that are not server-class.

`-Xmx[bytes]`

Overrides the maximum heap size in bytes. Default: Smaller than 1/4 physical memory or 1 GB. Maximum heap size is 64 MB for machines that are not server-class.

`-Xmn[bytes]`

The size of the heap for the young generation.

```
-XX:OnError=[command_line_tool [__options__]]
```
   Used to specify user-supplied scripts or commands when a
   fatal error occurs.

```
-XX+AggressiveOpts
```
   Enables performance optimizations that are expected to be
   on by default in future releases.

For a more complete list of options, visit Java HotSpot VM
Options (*http://bit.ly/16mhL27*). Java 9 validates command-line
flags to avoid crashes.

---

### TIP

Byte values include [k|K] for kilobytes, [m|M] for mega-
bytes, and [g|G] for gigabytes.

---

Note that -XX options are not guaranteed to be stable. They are
not part of the Java Language Specification (JLS) and are
unlikely to be available in exact form and function from other
third-party JVMs, if at all.

# Resizing the JVM Heap

The heap is an area in memory that stores all objects created by
executing a Java program. You should resize the heap only if it
needs to be sized larger than the default heap size. If you are
having performance problems or seeing the Permanent Generation (PermGen) error message `java.lang.OutOfMemoryError`,
you may be running out of heap space.

# Metaspace

Native memory is used for the representation of class metadata,
creating a memory space called *Metaspace*. Metaspace is the
sucessor to the PermGen model. Because of this, the JDK 8
HotSpot JVM will no longer see any PermGen `OutOfMemoryEr`

ror occurring. JVisualVM, prior to Java 9, provides analysis support to the Metaspace if any memory leaks should occur. JVisualVM is now VisualVM maintained on GitHub (*https://visualvm.github.io/*).

# Interfacing with the GC

Interfacing with the garbage collector can be done through explicit invocation or via overriding the `finalize` method.

## Explicit Garbage Collection

The garbage collector can be explicitly requested to be invoked with `System.gc()` or `Runtime.getRuntime().gc()`. However, explicit invocation of the GC should generally be avoided because it could force full collections (when a minor collection may suffice), thereby unnecessarily increasing the pause times. The request for `System.gc()` is not always fulfilled as the JVM can and does ignore it at times.

## Finalization

Every object has a `finalize()` method inherited from class `Object`. The garbage collector, prior to destroying the object, can invoke this method, but this invocation is not guaranteed. The default implementation of the `finalize()` method does nothing, and although it is not recommended, the method can be overridden:

```
public class TempClass extends SuperClass {
  ...
  // Performed when garbage collection occurs
  protected void finalize() throws Throwable {
    try {
      /* Desired functionality goes here */
    } finally {
      // Optionally, you can call the
      // finalize method of the superclass
      super.finalize(); // From SuperClass
    }
```

```
    }
  }
```

The following example destroys an object:

```
public class MainClass {
  public static void main(String[] args) {
    TempClass t = new TempClass();
    // Object has references removed
    t = null;
    // GC made available
    System.gc();
  }
}
```

CHAPTER 12
# Basic Input and Output

Java provides several classes for basic input and output, a few of which are discussed in this chapter. The basic classes can be used to read and write to files, sockets, and the console. They also provide for working with files and directories and for serializing data. Java I/O classes throw exceptions, including the IOException, which needs to be handled.

Java I/O classes also support formatting data, compressing and decompressing streams, encrypting and decrypting, and communicating between threads using piped streams.

The new I/O (NIO) APIs that were introduced in Java 1.4 provide additional I/O capabilities, including buffering, file locking, regular expression matching, scalable networking, and buffer management.

NIO.2 was introduced with Java SE 7 and is covered in the next chapter. NIO.2 extends NIO and provides a new filesystem API.

## Standard Streams in, out, and err

Java uses three standard streams: in, out, and err.

`System.in` is the standard input stream that is used to get data from the user to a program:

```
byte teamName[] = new byte[200];
int size = System.in.read(teamName);
System.out.write(teamName,0,size);
```

`System.out` is the standard output stream that is used to output data from a program to the user:

```
System.out.print("Team complete");
```

`System.err` is the standard error stream that is used to output error data from a program to the user:

```
System.err.println("Not enough players");
```

Note that each of these methods can throw an `IOException`.

---

### TIP

The `Console` class, introduced in Java SE 6, provides an alternative to the standard streams for interacting with the command-line environment.

---

# Class Hierarchy for Basic Input and Output

Figure 12-1 shows a class hierarchy for commonly used readers, writers, and input and output streams. Note that I/O classes can be chained together to get multiple effects.

The `Reader` and `Writer` classes are used for reading and writing character data (text). The `InputStream` and `OutputStream` classes are typically used for reading and writing binary data.

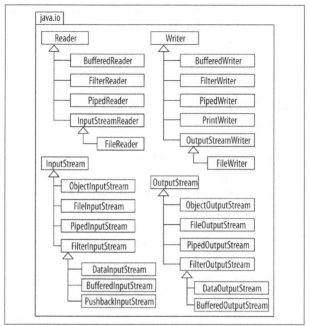

*Figure 12-1. Common readers, writers, and input/output streams*

# File Reading and Writing

Java provides facilities to easily read and write to system files.

## Reading Character Data from a File

To read character data from a file, use a BufferedReader. A File
Reader can also be used, but it will not be as efficient if there is
a large amount of data. The call to readLine() reads a line of
text from the file. When reading is complete, call close() on
the BufferedReader:

```
BufferedReader bReader = new BufferedReader
    (new FileReader("Master.txt"));
String lineContents;
```

```
while ((lineContents = bReader.readLine())
        != null) {...}
bReader.close();
```

Use NIO 2.0's `Files.newBufferedReader(<path>,<charset>);` to avoid the implicit assumption about the file encoding.

## Reading Binary Data from a File

To read binary data, use a `DataInputStream`. The call to `read()` reads the data from the input stream. Note that if only an array of bytes will be read, you should just use `InputStream`:

```
DataInputStream inStream = new DataInputStream
        (new FileInputStream("Team.bin"));
inStream.read();
```

If a large amount of data is going to be read, you should also use a `BufferedInputStream` to make reading the data more efficient:

```
DataInputStream inStream = new DataInputStream
(new BufferedInputStream(new FileInput
Stream(team)));
```

Binary data that has been read can be put back on the stream using methods in the `PushbackInputStream` class:

```
unread(int i);    // pushback a single byte
unread(byte[] b); // pushback array of bytes
```

## Writing Character Data to a File

To write character data to a file, use a `PrintWriter`. Call the `close()` method of class `PrintWriter` when writing to the output stream is complete:

```
String in = "A huge line of text";
PrintWriter pWriter = new PrintWriter
  (new FileWriter("CoachList.txt"));
pWriter.println(in);
pWriter.close();
```

Text can also be written to a file using a `FileWriter` if there is only a small amount of text to be written. Note that if the file passed into the `FileWriter` does not exist, it will automatically be created:

```
FileWriter fWriter = new
  FileWriter("CoachList.txt");
fWriter.write("This is the coach list.");
fWriter.close();
```

## Writing Binary Data to a File

To write binary data, use a `DataOutputStream`. The call to `write Int()` writes an array of integers to the output stream:

```
File positions = new File("Positions.bin");
int[] pos = {0, 1, 2, 3, 4};
DataOutputStream outStream = new DataOutputStream
  (new FileOutputStream(positions));
for (int i = 0; i < pos.length; i++)
  outStream.writeInt(pos[i]);
```

If a large amount of data is going to be written, then also use a `BufferedOutputStream`:

```
DataOutputStream outStream = new DataOutputStream
(new BufferedOutputStream(positions));
```

# Socket Reading and Writing

Java provides facilities to read and write to system sockets with ease.

## Reading Character Data from a Socket

To read character data from a socket, connect to the socket and then use a `BufferedReader` to read the data:

```
Socket socket = new Socket("127.0.0.1", 64783);
InputStreamReader reader = new InputStreamReader
  (socket.getInputStream());
BufferedReader bReader
```

```
   = new BufferedReader(reader);
String msg = bReader.readLine();
```

BufferedReader introduced the lines() method in Java SE 8, relative to the new Stream API. This method returns a Stream, the elements of which are lines lazily read from the contexted BufferedReader.

## Reading Binary Data from a Socket

To read binary data, use a DataInputStream. The call to read() reads the data from the input stream. Note that the Socket class is located in java.net:

```
Socket socket = new Socket("127.0.0.1", 64783);
DataInputStream inStream = new DataInputStream
   (socket.getInputStream());
inStream.read();
```

If a large amount of data is going to be read, then also use a BufferedInputStream to make reading the data more efficient:

```
DataInputStream inStream = new DataInputStream
(new BufferedInputStream(socket.getInputStream()));
```

## Writing Character Data to a Socket

To write character data to a socket, make a connection to a socket and then create and use a PrintWriter to write the character data to the socket:

```
Socket socket = new Socket("127.0.0.1", 64783);
PrintWriter pWriter = new PrintWriter
   (socket.getOutputStream());
pWriter.println("Dad, we won the game.");
```

## Writing Binary Data to a Socket

To write binary data, use a DataOutputStream. The call to write() writes the data to an output stream:

```
byte positions[] = new byte[10];
Socket socket = new Socket("127.0.0.1", 64783);
```

```
DataOutputStream outStream = new DataOutputStream
  (socket.getOutputStream());
outStream.write(positions, 0, 10);
```

If a large amount of data is going to be written, then also use a
BufferedOutputStream:

```
DataOutputStream outStream = new DataOutputStream
(new BufferedOutputStream(socket.getOutput
Stream()));
```

# Serialization

To save a version of an object (and all related data that would
need to be restored) as an array of bytes, the class of this object
must implement the interface Serializable. Note that data
members declared transient will not be included in the serial-
ized object. Use caution when using serialization and deseriali-
zation, as changes to a class—including moving the class in the
class hierarchy, deleting a field, changing a field to nontransient
or static, and using different JVMs—can all impact restoring an
object.

The ObjectOutputStream and ObjectInputStream classes can be
used to serialize and deserialize objects.

## Serialize

To serialize an object, use an ObjectOutputStream:

```
ObjectOutputStream s = new
  ObjectOutputStream(new FileOutput
Stream("p.ser"));
```

An example of serializing follows:

```
ObjectOutputStream oStream = new
  ObjectOutputStream(new
  FileOutputStream("PlayerDat.ser"));
oStream.writeObject(player);
oStream.close();
```

## Deserialize

To deserialize an object (i.e., turn it from a flattened version of an object to an object), use an ObjectInputStream; then read in the file and cast the data into the appropriate object:

```
ObjectInputStream d = new
    ObjectInputStream(new FileInputStream("p.ser"));
```

An example of deserializing follows:

```
ObjectInputStream iStream = new
    ObjectInputStream(new
    FileInputStream("PlayerDat.ser"));
Player p = (Player) iStream.readObject();
```

Java 9 allows incoming streams of object-serialization data to be filtered for security and robustness.

# Zipping and Unzipping Files

Java provides classes for creating compressed ZIP and GZIP files. ZIP archives multiple files, whereas GZIP archives a single file.

Use ZipOutputStream to zip files and ZipInputSteam to unzip them:

```
ZipOutputStream zipOut = new ZipOutputStream(
    new FileOutputStream("out.zip"));
String[] fNames = new String[] {"f1", "f2"};
for (int i = 0; i < fNames.length; i++) {
ZipEntry entry = new ZipEntry(fNames[i]);
FileInputStream fin =
    new FileInputStream(fNames[i]);
try {
  zipOut.putNextEntry(entry);
  for (int a = fin.read();
    a != -1; a = fin.read()) {
      zipOut.write(a);
  }
  fin.close();
```

```
    zipOut.close();
  }  catch (IOException ioe) {...}
}
```

To unzip a file, create a ZipInputStream, call its getNextEntry() method, and read the file into an OutputStream.

## Compressing and Uncompressing GZIP Files

To compress a GZIP file, create a new GZIPOutputStream, pass it the name of a file with the *.gzip* extension, and then transfer the data from the GZIPOutputStream to the FileInputStream.

To uncompress a GZIP file, create a GZipInputStream, create a new FileOutputStream, and read the data into it.

# CHAPTER 13

# New I/O API (NIO.2)

NIO.2 was introduced with JDK 7 to provide enhanced file I/O support and access to the default filesystem. NIO.2 is supported by the `java.nio.file` and `java.nio.file.attribute` packages. The NIO.2 API is also known as *JSR 203: More New I/O APIs for the Java Platform*. Popular interfaces that are used from the API are `Path`, `PathMatcher`, `FileVisitor`, and `WatchService`. Popular classes that are used from the API are `Paths` and `Files`.

## The Path Interface

The `Path` interface can be used to operate on file and directory paths. This class is an upgraded version of the `java.io.File` class. The following code demonstrates the use of some of the methods of the `Path` interface and the `Paths` class for acquiring information:

```
Path p = Paths.get("\\opt\\jpgTools\\README.txt");
System.out.println(p.getParent()); // \opt\jpgTools
System.out.println(p.getRoot()); // \
System.out.println(p.getNameCount()); // 3
System.out.println(p.getName(0)); // opt
System.out.println(p.getName(1)); // jpgTools
System.out.println(p.getFileName()); // README.txt
System.out.println(p.toString()); // The full path
```

The Path class also provides additional features, some of which are detailed in Table 13-1.

*Table 13-1. Path interface capabilities*

| Path method | Capability |
|---|---|
| path.toUri() | Converts a path to a URI object |
| path.resolve(*Path*) | Combines two paths together |
| path.relativize(*Path*) | Constructs a path from one location to another |
| path.compareTo(*Path*) | Compares two paths against each other |

## The Files Class

The Files class can be used to create, check, delete, copy, or move a file or directory. The following code demonstrates some commonly used methods of the Files class:

```
// Create directory
Path dirs = Paths.get("\\opt\\jpg\\");
Files.createDirectories(dirs);
// Instantiate path objects
Path target1 = Paths.get("\\opt\\jpg\
\README1.txt");
Path p1 = Files.createFile(target1);
Path target2 = Paths.get("\\opt\\jpg\
\README2.txt");
Path p2 = Files.createFile(target2);
// Check file attributes
System.out.println(Files.isReadable(p1));
System.out.println(Files.isReadable(p2));
System.out.println(Files.isExecutable(p1));
System.out.println(Files.isSymbolicLink(p1));
System.out.println(Files.isWritable(p1));
System.out.println(Files.isHidden(p1));
System.out.println(Files.isSameFile(p1, p2));

// Delete, move, and copy examples
Files.delete(p2);
System.out.println(Files.move(p1, p2));
```

```
System.out.println(Files.copy(p2, p1));
Files.delete(p1);
Files.delete(p2);
```

The move method accepts the varargs enumeration using REPLACE_EXISTING or ATOMIC_MOVE. REPLACE_EXISTING moves the file, even if it already exists. ATOMIC_MOVE ensures that any process watching the directory will be able to access the complete file.

The copy method accepts the varargs enumeration with REPLACE_EXISTING, COPY_ATTRIBUTES, or NOFOLLOW_LINKS. REPLACE_EXISTING copies the file, even if it already exists. COPY_ATTRIBUTES copies the file attributes. NOFOLLOW_LINKS copies the links, but not the targets.

The lines, list, walk, and find methods have been added to the Files class relative to the Stream API. The lines method lazily reads a stream of lines. The list method lazily lists directory entries, and walk recursively traverses the entries. The find method lazily provides Path by searching for files in a file tree rooted at a given file node.

# Additional Features

The NIO 2.0 API also provides the following features, which are good to know for the job. Questions about these features are also included on the Oracle Certified Professional Java SE 7 Programmer Exam. These items are not covered here, as they are more suited to a tutorial style guide or resource:

- The ability to watch a directory using the WatchService interface.
- The ability to recursively access directory trees using the FileVisitor interface.
- The ability to find files using the PathMatcher functional interface.

Since PathMatcher is a functional interface, it may be used with a lambda expression:

```
PathMatcher matcher = (Path p) -> {
  // returns boolean
  return (p.toString().contains("World"));
};
Path path1 = FileSystems.getDefault().getPath(
  "\\tmp\\Hello.java");
Path path2 = FileSystems.getDefault().getPath(
  "\\tmp\\HelloWorld.java");
System.out.print("Matches: "
  + matcher.matches(path1) + ", "
  + matcher.matches(path2));

$ Matches: false, true
```

---

### TIP

Consider using the new java.nio.file.Directory Stream functional interface with the enhanced for loop to iterate over a directory.

---

# CHAPTER 14

# Concurrency

Threads in Java allow the use of multiple processors or multiple cores in one processor to be more efficient. On a single processor, threads provide for concurrent operations such as overlapping I/O with processing.

Java supports multithreaded programming features with the Thread class and the Runnable interface.

## Creating Threads

Threads can be created two ways, either by extending java.lang.Thread or by implementing java.lang.Runnable.

### Extending the Thread Class

Extending the Thread class and overriding the run() method can create a threadable class. This is an easy way to start a thread:

```java
class Comet extends Thread {
  public void orbit() {
    System.out.println("orbiting");
  }
  public void run() {
    orbit();
```

```
    }
  }

  Comet halley = new Comet();
  halley.start();
```

Remember that only one superclass can be extended, so a class
that extends Thread cannot extend any other superclass.

## Implementing the Runnable Interface

Implementing the Runnable functional interface and defining
its run() method can also create a threadable class:

```
  class Asteroid implements Runnable {
    public void orbit() {
      System.out.println("orbiting");
    }
    public void run() {
      orbit();
    }
  }

  Asteroid majaAsteroid = new Asteroid();
  Thread majaThread = new Thread(majaAsteroid);
  majaThread.start();
```

A single runnable instance can be passed to multiple thread
objects. Each thread performs the same task, as shown here
after the use of a lambda expression:

```
  Runnable asteroid = () -> {
    System.out.println("orbiting");
  };
  Thread asteroidThread1 = new Thread(asteroid);
  Thread asteroidThread2 = new Thread(asteroid);
  asteroidThread1.start();
  asteroidThread2.start();
```

# Thread States

Enumeration `Thread.state` provides six thread states, as depicted in Table 14-1.

*Table 14-1. Thread states*

| Thread state | Description |
|---|---|
| NEW | A thread that is created but not started |
| RUNNABLE | A thread that is available to run |
| BLOCKED | An "alive" thread that is blocked waiting for a monitor lock |
| WAITING | An "alive" thread that calls its own `wait()` or `join()` while waiting on another thread |
| TIMED_WAITING | An "alive" thread that is waiting on another thread for a specified period of time; sleeping |
| TERMINATED | A thread that has completed |

# Thread Priorities

The valid range of priority values is typically 1 through 10, with a default value of 5. Thread priorities are one of the least portable aspects of Java, as their range and default values can vary among Java Virtual Machines (JVMs). Using `MIN_PRIORITY`, `NORM_PRIORITY`, and `MAX_PRIORITY` can retrieve priorities:

```
System.out.print(Thread.MAX_PRIORITY);
```

Lower-priority threads yield to higher-priority threads.

# Common Methods

Table 14-2 contains common methods used for threads from the `Thread` class.

*Table 14-2. Thread methods*

| Method | Description |
|--------|-------------|
| getPriority() | Returns the thread's priority |
| getState() | Returns the thread's state |
| interrupt() | Interrupts the thread |
| isAlive() | Returns the thread's alive status |
| isInterrupted() | Checks for interruption of the thread |
| join() | Causes the thread that invokes this method to wait for the thread that this object represents to finish |
| setPrior ity(int) | Sets the thread's priority |
| start() | Places the thread into a runnable state |

Table 14-3 contains common methods used for threads from the Object class.

*Table 14-3. Methods from the Object class used for threads*

| Method | Description |
|--------|-------------|
| notify() | Tells a thread to wake up and run |
| noti fyAll() | Tells all threads that are waiting on a thread or resource to wake up, and then the scheduler will select one of the threads to run |
| wait() | Pauses a thread in a wait state until another thread calls notify() or notifyAll() |

---

### TIP

Calls to wait() and notify() throw an Interrupted Exception if called on a thread that has its interrupted flag set to true.

---

Table 14-4 contains common static methods used for threads from the Thread class (i.e., Thread.sleep(1000)).

*Table 14-4. Static thread methods*

| Method | Description |
|--------|-------------|
| activeCount() | Returns number of threads in the current thread's group |
| currentTh read() | Returns reference to the currently running thread |
| interrupted() | Checks for interruption of the currently running thread |
| sleep(long) | Blocks the currently running thread for +*parameter*+ number of milliseconds |
| yield() | Pauses the current thread to allow other threads to run |

## Synchronization

The synchronized keyword provides a means to apply locks to blocks and methods. Locks should be applied to blocks and methods that access critically shared resources. These monitor locks begin and end with opening and closing braces. Following are some examples of synchronized blocks and methods.

Object instance t with a synchronized lock:

```
synchronized (t) {
  // Block body
}
```

Object instance this with a synchronized lock:

```
synchronized (this) {
  // Block body
}
```

Method raise() with a synchronized lock:

```
// Equivalent code segment 1
synchronized void raise() {
  // Method body
}
```

```
// Equivalent code segment 2
void raise() {
  synchronized (this) {
    // Method body
  }
}
```

Static method `calibrate()` with a synchronized lock:

```
class Telescope {
  synchronized static void calibrate() {
    // Method body
  }
}
```

---

**TIP**

A lock is also known as a *monitor* or *mutex* (mutually exclusive lock).

---

The concurrent utilities provide additional means to apply and manage concurrency.

# Concurrent Utilities

Java 2 SE 5.0 introduced utility classes for concurrent programming. These utilities reside in the `java.util.concurrent` package, and they include executors, concurrent collections, synchronizers, and timing utilities.

## Executors

The class `ThreadPoolExecutor`, as well as its subclass `Scheduled ThreadPoolExecutor`, implement the `Executor` interface to provide configurable, flexible thread pools. Thread pools allow server components to take advantage of the reusability of threads.

The class Executors provides factory (object creator) methods and utility methods. Of them, the following are supplied to create thread pools:

newCachedThreadPool()
> Creates an unbounded thread pool that automatically reuses threads

newFixedThreadPool(int nThreads)
> Creates a fixed-size thread pool that automatically reuses threads off a shared unbounded queue

newScheduledThreadPool(int corePoolSize)
> Creates a thread pool that can have commands scheduled to run periodically or on a specified delay

newSingleThreadExecutor()
> Creates a single-threaded executor that operates off an unbounded queue

newSingleThreadScheduledExecutor()
> Creates a single-threaded executor that can have commands scheduled to run periodically or by a specified delay

The following example demonstrates usage of the newFixed ThreadPool factory method:

```
import java.util.concurrent.Executors;
import java.util.concurrent.ExecutorService;

public class ThreadPoolExample {
  public static void main() {
    // Create tasks
    // (from 'class RTask implements Runnable')
    RTask t1 = new RTask("thread1");
    RTask t2 = new RTask("thread2");

    // Create thread manager
    ExecutorService threadExecutor =
        Executors.newFixedThreadPool(2);
```

```
    // Make threads runnable
    threadExecutor.execute(t1);
    threadExecutor.execute(t2);

    // Shut down threads
    threadExecutor.shutdown();
  }
}
```

## Concurrent Collections

Even though collection types can be synchronized, it is best to use concurrent thread-safe classes that perform equivalent functionality, as represented in Table 14-5.

*Table 14-5. Collections and their thread-safe equivalents*

| Collection class | Thread-safe equivalent |
|---|---|
| HashMap | ConcurrentHashMap |
| TreeMap | ConcurrentSkipListMap |
| TreeSet | ConcurrentSkipListSet |
| Map subtypes | ConcurrentMap |
| List subtypes | CopyOnWriteArrayList |
| Set subtypes | CopyOnWriteArraySet |
| PriorityQueue | PriorityBlockingQueue |
| Deque | BlockingDeque |
| Queue | BlockingQueue |

## Synchronizers

Synchronizers are special-purpose synchronization tools. Available synchronizers are listed in Table 14-6.

*Table 14-6. Synchronizers*

| Synchronizer | Description |
|---|---|
| Semaphore | Maintains a set of permits |

| Synchronizer | Description |
| --- | --- |
| CountDown Latch | Implements waits against sets of operations being performed |
| CyclicBarrier | Implements waits against common barrier points |
| Exchanger | Implements a synchronization point where threads can exchange elements |

## Timing Utility

The TimeUnit enumeration is commonly used to inform time-based methods how a given timing parameter should be evaluated, as shown in the following example:

```
// tyrLock (long time, TimeUnit unit)
if (lock.tryLock(15L, TimeUnit.DAYS)) {...}
  //15 days
```

Available TimeUnit enum constants are listed in Table 14-7.

*Table 14-7. TimeUnit constants*

| Constants | Unit def. | Unit (sec) | Abbreviation |
| --- | --- | --- | --- |
| NANOSECONDS | 1/1000 µs | .000000001 | ns |
| MICROSECONDS | 1/1000 ms | .000001 | µs |
| MILLISECONDS | 1/1000 sec | .001 | ms |
| SECONDS | sec | 1 | sec |
| MINUTES | 60 sec | 60 | min |
| HOURS | 60 min | 3,600 | hr |
| DAYS | 24 hr | 86,400 | d |

# CHAPTER 15

# Java Collections Framework

The Java Collections Framework is designed to support numerous collections in a hierarchical fashion. It is essentially made up of interfaces, implementations, and algorithms.

## The Collection Interface

*Collections* are objects that group multiple elements and store, retrieve, and manipulate those elements. The Collection interface is at the root of the collection hierarchy. Subinterfaces of Collection include List, Queue, and Set. Table 15-1 shows these interfaces and whether they are ordered or allow duplicates. The Map interface is also included in the table, as it is part of the framework.

*Table 15-1. Common collections*

| Interface | Ordered | Dupes | Notes |
|-----------|---------|-------|-------|
| List | Yes | Yes | Positional access; element insertion control |
| Map | Can be | No (Keys) | Unique keys; one value mapping max per key |
| Queue | Yes | Yes | Holds elements; usually FIFO |
| Set | Can be | No | Uniqueness matters |

# Implementations

Table 15-2 lists commonly used collection type implementations, their interfaces, and whether or not they are ordered, sorted, and/or contain duplicates.

*Table 15-2. Collection type implementations*

| Implementations | Interface | Ordered | Sorted | Dupes | Notes |
|---|---|---|---|---|---|
| ArrayList | List | Index | No | Yes | Fast resizable array |
| LinkedList | List | Index | No | Yes | Doubly linked list |
| Vector | List | Index | No | Yes | Legacy, synchronized |
| HashMap | Map | No | No | No | Key/value pairs |
| Hashtable | Map | No | No | No | Legacy, synchronized |
| LinkedHash Map | Map | Insertion, last access | No | No | Linked list/hash table |
| TreeMap | Map | Balanced | Yes | No | Red-black tree map |
| Priority Queue | Queue | Priority | Yes | Yes | Heap implementation |
| HashSet | Set | No | No | No | Fast access set |
| LinkedHash Set | Set | Insertion | No | No | Linked list/hash set |
| TreeSet | Set | Sorted | Yes | No | Red-black tree set |

# Collection Framework Methods

The subinterfaces of the Collection interface provide several valuable method signatures, as shown in Table 15-3.

*Table 15-3. Valuable subinterface methods*

| Method | List params | Set params | Map params | Returns |
|---|---|---|---|---|
| add | index, element | element | n/a | boolean |
| contains | Object | Object | n/a | boolean |
| containsKey | n/a | n/a | key | boolean |
| containsValue | n/a | n/a | value | boolean |
| get | index | n/a | key | Object |
| indexOf | Object | n/a | n/a | int |
| iterator | none | none | n/a | Iterator |
| keySet | n/a | n/a | none | Set |
| put | n/a | n/a | key, value | void |
| remove | index or Object | Object | key | void |
| size | none | none | none | int |

Collection.stream() returns a sequential Stream with the context collection as its source. Collection.parallelStream() returns a parallel Stream with the context collection as its source.

# Collections Class Algorithms

The Collections class, not to be confused with the Collection interface, contains several valuable static methods (e.g., algorithms). These methods can be invoked on a variety of collection types. Table 15-4 shows commonly used Collection class methods, their acceptable parameters, and return values.

*Table 15-4. Collection class algorithms*

| Method | Parameters | Returns |
|---|---|---|
| addAll | Collection <? super T>, T... | boolean |
| max | Collection, [Comparator] | <T> |
| min | Collection, [Comparator] | <T> |
| disjoint | Collection, Collection | boolean |
| frequency | Collection, Object | int |
| asLifoQueue | Deque | Queue<T> |
| reverse | List | void |
| shuffle | List | void |
| copy | List destination, List source | void |
| rotate | List, int distance | void |
| swap | List, int position, int position | void |
| binarySearch | List, Object | int |
| fill | List, Object | void |
| sort | List, Object, [Comparator] | void |
| replaceAll | List, Object oldValue, Object newValue | boolean |
| newSetFromMap | Map | Set<E> |

See Chapter 16 for more information on typed parameters (e.g., <T>).

## Algorithm Efficiencies

Algorithms and data structures are optimized for different reasons—some for random element access or insertion/deletion, others for keeping things in order. Depending on your needs, you may have to switch algorithms and structures.

Common collection algorithms, their types, and average time efficiencies are shown in Table 15-5.

*Table 15-5. Algorithm efficiencies*

| Algorithms | Concrete type | Time |
|---|---|---|
| get, set | ArrayList | O(1) |
| add, remove | ArrayList | O(n) |
| contains, indexOf | ArrayList | O(n) |
| get, put, remove, containsKey | HashMap | O(1) |
| add, remove, contains | HashSet | O(1) |
| add, remove, contains | LinkedHash Set | O(1) |
| get, set, add, remove (from either end) | LinkedList | O(1) |
| get, set, add, remove (from index) | LinkedList | O(n) |
| contains, indexOf | LinkedList | O(n) |
| peek | Priority Queue | O(1) |
| add, remove | Priority Queue | O(log n) |
| remove, get, put, containsKey | TreeMap | O(log n) |
| add, remove, contains | TreeSet | O(log n) |

The Big O notation is used to indicate time efficiencies, where *n* is the number of elements (see Table 15-6).

*Table 15-6. Big O notation*

| Notation | Description |
|---|---|
| O(1) | Time is constant, regardless of the number of elements. |
| O(n) | Time is linear to the number of elements. |
| O(log n) | Time is logarithmic to the number of elements. |
| O(n log n) | Time is linearithmic to the number of elements. |

# Comparator Functional Interface

Several methods in the Collections class assume that the objects in the collection are comparable. If there is no natural ordering, a helper class can implement the Comparator functional interface to specify how the objects are to be ordered. The code example here orders surnames by their generated metaphone codes:

---

### TIP

Take a look at the Metaphone Code Calculator written with Java for a better understanding of metaphone codes.

---

```java
import org.apache.commons.codec.language.Metaphone;
public class MetaphoneCode {
  private String metaphoneCode;
  public MetaphoneCode(String surname) {
    Metaphone m = new Metaphone();
    metaphoneCode = m.metaphone(surname) + "(" +
surname + ")";
  }
  public String getMetaphoneCode() {
    return metaphoneCode;
  }
  public void setMetaphoneCode(String metaphone
Code) {
    this.metaphoneCode = metaphoneCode;
  }
  public String toString() {
    return this.metaphoneCode;
  }
}

import java.util.Comparator;
public class SurnameSort implements Comparator <Met
aphoneCode> {
  @Override
```

```
   public int compare (MetaphoneCode mc1, Metaphone
Code mc2) {
    return mc1.getMetaphoneCode().compareTo(mc2.get
MetaphoneCode());
  }
}

import java.util.ArrayList;
import java.util.Collections;
public class SurnameApp {
  public static void main(String[] args) {
    MetaphoneCode m1 = new Metaphone
Code("Whitede");
    MetaphoneCode m2 = new MetaphoneCode("White
head");
    MetaphoneCode m3 = new MetaphoneCode("Whit
ted");
    MetaphoneCode m4 = new MetaphoneCode("Whits
head");
    MetaphoneCode m5 = new MetaphoneCode("White");
    ArrayList<MetaphoneCode> mlist = new ArrayList
<>();
    mList.add(m1);
    mList.add(m2);
    mList.add(m3);
    mList.add(m4);
    mList.add(m5);
    System.out.println("Unsorted: " + mList );
    SurnameSort cSort = new SurnameSort();
    Collections.sort(mList, cSort);
    System.out.println("Sorted: " + mList );
  }
}

$ Unsorted: [WTT (Whitede), WTHT( Whitehead), WTT
(Whitted), WTXT (Whitshead), WT (White)]
$ Sorted: [WT (White), WTHT (Whitehead), WTT
(Whitede), WTT (Whitted), WTXT (Whitshead)]
```

The SurnameSort class implemented the Comparator interface
that was used by the cSort instance. Optionally, an anonymous

inner class could have been created to avoid the work of creating the seperate SurnameSort class:

```
// Replace: SurnameSort cSort = new SurnameSort();
Comparator<MetaphoneCode> cSort = new Compara
tor<MetaphoneCode>() {
  public int compare(MetaphoneCode mc1, Metaphone
Code mc2) {
    return mc1.getMetaphoneCode().compareTo(mc2.get
MetaphoneCode());
  }
};
```

Since Comparator is a functional interface, a lambda expression could have been used to make the code more readable:

```
Comparator<MetaphoneCode> cSort = (MetaphoneCode
mc1, MetaphoneCode mc2)
  -> mc1.getMetaphoneCode().compareTo(mc2.getMeta
phoneCode());
```

Class names do not need to be explicitly stated in the argument list, as the lambda expressions have knowledge of the target types. That is, notice (mc1, mc2) versus (MetaphoneCode mc1, MetaphoneCode mc2):

```
// Example 1
Comparator <MetaphoneCode> cSort = (mc1, mc2)
  -> mc1.getMetaphoneCode().compareTo(mc2.getMeta
phoneCode());
Collections.sort(mList, cSort);

// Example 2
Collections.sort(mList, (mc1, mc2)
  -> mc1.getMetaphoneCode().compareTo(mc2.getMetapho
neCode()));
```

# Convenience Factory Methods

JDK 9 introduces new convenience factory methods that create compact unmodifiable collection (e.g., List, Set, Map) instances. Therefore, multiple lines of code can be refactored into one:

```
// Pre Java 9 immutable list instantiation
List<String> haplogroups = new ArrayList<>();
haplogroups.add("I2");
haplogroups.add("I2B");
haplogroups.add("IJ");
haplogroups = Collections.unmodifiableList(hap
logroups);

// Refactored Java 9 immutable list instantiation
List <String> haplogroups = List.of("I2","I2B",
"IJ");
```

**CHAPTER 16**

# Generics Framework

The Generics Framework, introduced in Java SE 5.0 and updated in Java SE 7 and 8, provides support that allows for the parameterization of types. Generics over Primitive Types is targeted for Java SE 10.

The benefit of generics is the significant reduction in the amount of code that needs to be written when developing a library. Another benefit is the elimination of casting in many situations.

The classes of the Collections Framework, the class Class, and other Java libraries have been updated to include generics.

See *Java Generics and Collections (http://bit.ly/java-generics-collections)* by Philip Wadler and Maurice Naftalin (O'Reilly, 2009) for comprehensive coverage of the Generics Framework.

## Generic Classes and Interfaces

Generic classes and interfaces parameterize types by adding a type parameter within angular brackets (i.e., <T>). The type is instantiated at the place of the brackets.

Once instantiated, the generic parameter type is applied throughout the class for methods that have the same type specified. In the following example, the add() and get() methods use the parameterized type as their parameter argument and return types, respectively:

```
public interface List <E> extends Collection<E>{
  public boolean add(E e);
  E get(int index);
}
```

When a variable of a parameterized type is declared, a concrete type (i.e., <Integer>) is specified to be used in place of the type parameter (i.e., <E>).

Subsequently, the need to cast when retrieving elements from things such as collections would be eliminated:

```
// Collection List/ArrayList with generics
List<Integer> iList = new ArrayList<Integer>();
iList.add(1000);
// Explicit cast not necessary
Integer i = iList.get(0);

// Collection List/ArrayList without generics
List iList = new ArrayList();
iList.add(1000);
// Explicit cast is necessary
Integer i = (Integer)iList.get(0);
```

The diamond operator <> was introduced in Java SE 7 to simplify the creation of generic types, by reducing the need for additional typing:

```
// Without the use of the diamond operator
List<Integer> iList1 = new ArrayList<Integer>();
// With the use of the diamond operator
List<Integer> iList2 = new ArrayList<>();
```

## Constructors with Generics

Constructors of generic classes do not require generic type parameters as arguments:

```
// Generic class
public class SpecialList <E> {
  // Constructor without arguments
  public SpecialList() {...}
  public SpecialList(String s) {...}
}
```

A generic object of this class could be instantiated as such:

```
SpecialList<String> b = new
        SpecialList<String>();
```

If a constructor for a generic class includes a parameter type, such as a String, the generic object could be instantiated as such:

```
SpecialList<String> b = new
      SpecialList<String>("Joan Marie");
```

# Substitution Principle

As specified in *Java Generics and Collections* (O'Reilly), the substitution principle allows subtypes to be used where their supertype is parameterized:

- A variable of a given type may be assigned a value of any subtype of that type.

- A method with a parameter of a given type may be invoked with an argument of any subtype of that type.

Byte, Short, Integer, Long, Float, Double, BigInteger, and BigDecimal are all subtypes of class Number:

```
// List declared with generic Number type
List<Number> nList = new ArrayList<Number>();
nList.add((byte)27);      // Byte (Autoboxing)
```

```
nList.add((short)30000); // Short
nList.add(1234567890);    // Integer
nList.add((long)2e62);    // Long
nList.add((float)3.4);    // Float
nList.add(4000.8);        // Double
nList.add(new BigInteger("9223372036854775810"));
nList.add(new BigDecimal("2.1e309"));

// Print Number's subtype values from the list
for( Number n : nList )
  System.out.println(n);
```

# Type Parameters, Wildcards, and Bounds

The simplest declaration of a generic class is with an unbounded type parameter, such as T:

```
public class GenericClass <T> {...}
```

Bounds (constraints) and wildcards can be applied to the type parameter(s), as shown in Table 16-1.

*Table 16-1. Type parameters, bounds, and wildcards*

| Type parameters | Description |
| --- | --- |
| <T> | Unbounded type; same as <T extends Object> |
| <T,P> | Unbounded types; <T extends Object> and <P extends Object> |
| <T extends P> | Upper bounded type; a specific type T that is a subtype of type P |
| <T extends P & S> | Upper bounded type; a specific type T that is a subtype of type P and that implements type S |
| <T super P> | Lower bounded type; a specific type T that is a supertype of type P |
| <?> | Unbounded wildcard; any object type, same as <? extends Object> |
| <? extends P> | Bounded wildcard; some unknown type that is a subtype of type P |

| Type parameters | Description |
|---|---|
| <? extends P & S> | Bounded wildcard; some unknown type that is a subtype of type P and that implements type S |
| <? super P> | Lower bounded wildcard; some unknown type that is a supertype of type P |

# The Get and Put Principle

As also specified in *Java Generics and Collections*, the get and put principle details the best usage of extends and super wildcards:

- Use an extends wildcard when you get only values out of a structure.

- Use a super wildcard when you put only values into a structure.

- Do not use a wildcard when you place both get and put values into a structure.

The extends wildcard has been used in the method declaration of the addAll() method of the List collection, as this method *gets* values from a collection:

```
public interface List <E> extends Collection<E>{
  boolean addALL(Collection <? extends E> c)
}

List<Integer> srcList = new ArrayList<Integer>();
srcList.add(0);
srcList.add(1);
srcList.add(2);
// Using addAll() method with extends wildcard
List<Integer> destList = new ArrayList<Integer>();
destList.addAll(srcList);
```

The super wildcard has been used in the method declaration of the addAll() method of the class Collections, as the method *puts* values into a collection:

```
public class Collections {
  public static <T> boolean addAll
      (Collection<? super T> c, T... elements){...}
}

// Using addAll() method with super wildcard
List<Number> sList = new ArrayList<Number>();
sList.add(0);
Collections.addAll(sList, (byte)1, (short)2);
```

# Generic Specialization

A generic type can be extended in a variety of ways.

Given the parameterized abstract class AbstractSet <E>:

class SpecialSet<E> extends AbstractSet<E> {...}
> The SpecialSet class extends the AbstractSet class with the parameter type E. This is the typical way to declare generalizations with generics.

class SpecialSet extends AbstractSet<String> {...}
> The SpecialSet class extends the AbstractSet class with the parameterized type String.

class SpecialSet<E,P> extends AbstractSet<E> {...}
> The SpecialSet class extends the AbstractSet class with the parameter type E. Type P is unique to the SpecialSet class.

class SpecialSet<E> extends AbstractSet {...}
> The SpecialSet class is a generic class that would parameterize the generic type of the AbstractSet class. Because the raw type of the AbstractSet class has been extended (as opposed to generic), the parameterization cannot occur. Compiler warnings will be generated upon method invocation attempts.

class SpecialSet extends AbstractSet {...}
> The SpecialSet class extends the raw type of the Abstract Set class. Because the generic version of the AbstractSet

class was expected, compiler warnings will be generated upon method invocation attempts.

# Generic Methods in Raw Types

Static methods, nonstatic methods, and constructors that are part of nongeneric or raw type classes can be declared as generic. A raw type class is the nongeneric counterpart class to a generic class.

For generic methods of nongeneric classes, the method's return type must be preceded with the generic type parameter (e.g., <E>). However, there is no functional relationship between the type parameter and the return type, unless the return type is of the generic type:

```java
public class SpecialQueue {
  public static <E> boolean add(E e) {...}
  public static <E> E peek() {...}
}
```

When calling the generic method, the generic type parameter is placed before the method name. Here, <String> is used to specify the generic type argument:

```java
SpecialQueue.<String>add("White Carnation");
```

# CHAPTER 17

# The Java Scripting API

The Java Scripting API, introduced in Java SE 6, provides support that allows Java applications and scripting languages to interact through a standard interface. This API is detailed in JSR 223, "Scripting for the Java Platform," and is contained in the `javax.script` package found within the `java.scripting` module.

## Scripting Languages

Several scripting languages have script engine implementations available that conform to JSR 223. See "Scripting Languages Compatible with JSR-223" on page 242 in Appendix B for a subset of these supported languages.

## Script Engine Implementations

The `ScriptEngine` interface provides the fundamental methods for the API. The `ScriptEngineManager` class works in conjunction with this interface and provides a means to establish the desired scripting engines to be utilized.

## Embedding Scripts into Java

The scripting API includes the ability to embed scripts and/or scripting components into Java applications.

The following example shows two ways to embed scripting components into a Java application: (1) the scripting engine's eval method reads in the scripting language syntax directly, and (2) the scripting engine's eval method reads the syntax in from a file:

```
import java.io.FileReader;
import java.nio.file.Path;
import java.nio.file.Paths;
import javax.script.ScriptEngine;
import javax.script.ScriptEngineManager;

public class HelloWorld {
  public static void main(String[] args) throws
      Exception {
    ScriptEngineManager m
        = new ScriptEngineManager();
    // Sets up Nashorn JavaScript Engine
    ScriptEngine e = m.getEngineByExtension("js");
    // Nashorn JavaScript syntax
    e.eval("print ('Hello, ')");
    // world.js contents: print('World!\n');
    Path p1 = Paths.get("/opt/jpg2/world.js");
    e.eval(new FileReader(p1.toString()));
  }
}

$ Hello, World!
```

## Invoking Methods of Scripting Languages

Scripting engines that implement the optional Invocable interface provide a means to invoke (execute) scripting language methods that the engine has already evaluated (interpreted).

The following Java-based `invokeFunction()` method calls the evaluated Nashorn scripting language function `greet()`, which we have created:

```
ScriptEngineManager m = new ScriptEngineManager();
ScriptEngine e = m.getEngineByExtension("js");
e.eval("function greet(message) {print(message)}");
Invocable i = (Invocable) e;
i.invokeFunction("greet", "Greetings from Mars!");

$ Greetings from Mars!
```

## Accessing and Controlling Java Resources from Scripts

The Java Scripting API provides the ability to access and control Java resources (objects) from within evaluated scripting language code. The script engines use key-value bindings.

Here, the evaluated Nashorn JavaScript makes use of the name Key/world binding and reads in (and prints out) a Java data member from the evaluated scripting language:

```
ScriptEngineManager m = new ScriptEngineManager();
ScriptEngine e = m.getEngineByExtension("js");
e.put("nameKey", "Gliese 581 c");
e.eval("var w = nameKey" );
e.eval("print(w)");

$ Gliese 581 c
```

By utilizing the key-value bindings, you can make modifications to the Java data members from the evaluated scripting language:

```
ScriptEngineManager m = new ScriptEngineManager();
ScriptEngine e = m.getEngineByExtension("js");
List<String> worldList = new ArrayList<>();
worldList.add ("Earth");
worldList.add ("Mars");
e.put("nameKey", worldList);
e.eval("var w = nameKey.toArray();");
```

```
e.eval(" nameKey.add (\"Gliese 581 c\")");
System.out.println(worldList);

$ [Earth, Gliese 581 c]
```

# Setting Up Scripting Languages and Engines

Before using the Scripting API, you must obtain and set up the desired script engine implementations. Many scripting languages include the JSR-223 scripting engine with their distribution, either in a separate JAR or in their main JAR, as in the case of JRuby.

## Scripting Language Setup

Here are the steps for setting up the scripting language:

1. Set up the scripting language on your system. "Scripting Languages Compatible with JSR-223" on page 242 in Appendix B contains a list of download sites for some supported scripting languages. Follow the associated installation instructions.

2. Invoke the script interpreters to ensure that they function properly. There is normally a command-line interpreter, as well as one with a graphical user interface.

For JRuby (as an example), the following commands should be validated to ensure proper setup:

```
jruby [file.rb] //Command line file
jruby.bat //Windows batch file
```

## Scripting Engine Setup

Here are the steps for setting up the scripting engine:

1. Determine if your scripting language distribution includes the JSR-223 scripting API engine in its distribution. If it is included, steps 2 and 3 are not necessary.

2. Download the scripting engine file from the engine's website.

3. Place the downloaded file into a directory and extract it to expose the necessary JAR. Note that the optional software (*opt*) directory is commonly used as an installation directory.

---

**TIP**

To install and configure certain scripting languages on a Windows machine, you may need a minimal POSIX-compliant shell, such as MSYS or Cygwin.

---

## Scripting Engine Validation

Validate the scripting engine setup by compiling and/or interpreting the scripting language libraries and the scripting engine libraries. The following is an older version of JRuby where the engine was available externally:

```
javac -cp c:\opt\jruby-1.0\lib\jruby.jar;c:\opt\
jruby-engine.jar;. Engines
```

You can perform additional testing with short programs. The following application produces a list of the available scripting engine names, language version numbers, and extensions. Note that this updated version of JRuby includes JSR-223 support in its primary JAR file; therefore, the engine does not need to be separately called out on the class path:

```
$ java -cp c:\opt\jruby-9.1.6.0\lib\jruby.jar;.
  EngineReport

import java.util.List;
import javax.script.ScriptEngineManager;
import javax.script.ScriptEngineFactory;
```

```java
public class EngineReport {
  public static void main(String[] args) {
    ScriptEngineManager m =
        new ScriptEngineManager();
    List<ScriptEngineFactory> s =
        m.getEngineFactories();
    // Iterate through list of factories
    for (ScriptEngineFactory f: s) {
      // Release name and version
      String en = f.getEngineName();
      String ev = f.getEngineVersion();
      System.out.println("Engine: "
        + en + " " + ev);
      // Language name and version
      String ln = f.getLanguageName();
      String lv = f.getLanguageVersion();
      System.out.println("Language: "
        + ln + " " + lv);
      // Extensions
      List<String> l = f.getExtensions();
      for (String x: l) {
        System.out.println("Extensions: " + x);
      }
    }
  }
}

$ Engine: JSR 223 JRuby Engine 9.1.6.0
$ Language: ruby jruby 9.1.6.0
$ Extensions: rb

$ Engine: Oracle Nashorn 9-ea
$ Language: ECMAScript ECMA - 262 Edition 5.1
$ Extensions: js
```

**TIP**

Nashorn JavaScript is a scripting API packaged with Java SE 8 onwards. The command and argument `jjs -script ing` invokes the Nashorn engine with shell scripting features.

# CHAPTER 18

# Date and Time API

The Date and Time API (JSR 310) provides support for date, time, and calendar calculations. The reference implementation (RI) for this JSR is the ThreeTen Project (*http:// www.threeten.org/*) and was provided for inclusion into JDK 1.8. The Date and Time API is relative to the `java.time` package and the following subpackages: `java.time.chrono`, `java.time.format`, `java.time.temporal`, and `java.time.zone`.

JSR 310 achieved several design goals:

- A fluent API that is easy to read with chained methods
- A thread-safe design with immutable value classes
- An extensible API with calendar systems, adjusters, and queries
- Expectable behavior where each method's behavior is clear and well defined

The Date and Time API uses the International Organization for Standardization date and time data exchange model (ISO 8601). The ISO 8601 standard is formally called "Data elements and interchange formats—Information interchange—Representation of dates and times." The standard is based on the Gregorian calendar. Regional calendars are also supported.

See Appendix A for more information on fluent APIs.

## Legacy Interoperability

JSR 310 supercedes but does not deprecate java.util.Date, java.util.Calendar, java.util.DateFormat, java.util.Gregor ianCalendar, java.util.TimeZone, and java.sql.Date. JDK 8 provides methods to these classes to convert to and from the JSR 310 types for legacy support:

```
// Legacy Calendar -> New Instant-> Legacy Date
Calendar c = Calendar.getInstance();
Instant i =  c.toInstant();
Date d = Date.from(i);

/*
 * New ZonedDateTime -> Legacy GregorianCalendar
 * -> New LocalDateTime
 */
ZonedDateTime zdt =
  ZonedDateTime.parse("2014-02-24T11:17:00+01:00"
  + "[Europe/Gibraltar]")
GregorianCalendar gc = GregorianCalendar.from(zdt);
LocalDateTime ldt
  = gc.toZonedDateTime().toLocalDateTime();
```

## Regional Calendars

JSR 310 allows for the addition of new calendars. When creating a new calendar, classes need to be implemented against the Era, Chronology, and ChronoLocalDate interfaces.

Four regional calendars are packaged with the API:

- Hijrah
- Japanese imperial
- Minguo
- Thai Buddhist

---

With regional calendars, you will not be using the main classes of the ISO calendar.

# ISO Calendar

The primary java.time package of the API provides the ISO 8601 calendar system that is based on Gregorian rules. This and the related packages of the API provide an easy-to-use interface, as you can see in the following example of determining age difference between two dates. This example was derived from Gliesians Age Difference Calculator:

```
final String YANNI_BIRTH_YEAR = "1954";
final String ADELE_BIRTH_YEAR = "1988";

Year birthYear1 = Year.parse(YANNI_BIRTH_YEAR);
Year birthYear2 = Year.parse(ADELE_BIRTH_YEAR);
long diff
  = ChronoUnit.YEARS.between(birthYear1,
                            birthYear2);
System.out.println("There is an age difference of "
  + Math.abs(diff) + " years." );

$ There is an age difference of 34 years.
```

The primary classes of the API are listed here with key text derived from the online API:

Instant

Instantaneous point on the timeline. Measured from the standard Java epoch of 1970-01-01T00:00:00Z.

LocalDate

Immutable date-time object. *t* represents a date, viewed as year-month-day.

LocalTime

Immutable date-time object that represents a time. Viewed as hour-minute-second.

**LocalDateTime**

Immutable date-time object that represents a date-time. Viewed as year-month-day-hour-minute-second.

**OffsetTime**

Immutable date-time object that represents a time. Viewed as hour-minute-second-offset.

**OffsetDateTime**

Immutable representation of a date-time with an offset. Stores all date and time fields to a precision of nanoseconds, as well as the offset from UTC/Greenwich.

**ZonedDateTime**

Immutable representation of a date-time with a time zone. Stores all date and time fields to a precision of nanoseconds and a time zone, with a zone offset used to handle ambiguous local date-times.

**ZoneOffset**

Time-zone offset. Amount of time that a time-zone differs from Greenwich/UTC.

**ZonedId**

Time-zone identification. Used to identify the rules to convert between an Instant and a LocalDateTime.

**Year**

Immutable date-time object; represents a year.

**YearMonth**

Immutable date-time object. Represents the combination of a year and month.

**MonthDay**

Immutable date-time object. Represents the combination of a year and month.

**DayOfWeek**

Enumeration for the days of the week: Monday, Tuesday, Wednesday, Thursday, Friday, Saturday, and Sunday.

Month

Enumeration for the months of the year: January, February, March, April, May, June, July, August, September, October, November, and December.

Duration

A time-based amount of time measured in seconds.

Period

A date-based amount of time.

Clock

A clock provides access to the current instant, date, and time using a time zone. Its use is optional.

The sections that follow highlight key attributes and usage of some of these classes.

## Machine Interface

JSR 310 uses the UNIX Epoch for its default ISO 8301 calendar, with zero starting at 1970-01-01T00:00Z. Time is continuous since then, with negative values for instances before it.

To get an instance of the current time, simply call the Instant.now() method:

```
Instant i = Instant.now();

System.out.println("Machine: " + i.toEpochMilli());
$ Machine: 1478860514417

System.out.println("Human: " + i);
$ Human: 2016-11-11T10:35:31.727Z
```

The Clock class provides access to the current instant, date, and time while using a time zone:

```
Clock clock1 = Clock.systemUTC();
Instant i1 = Instant.now(clock1);

ZoneId zid = ZoneId.of("Europe/Vienna");
```

```
Clock clock2 = Clock.system(zid);
Instant i2 = Instant.now(clock2);
```

The Date-Time API uses the Time Zone Database (TZDB) (*http://www.iana.org/time-zones*).

## Durations and Periods

A Duration is a time-based amount consisting of days, hours, minutes, seconds, and nanoseconds. A duration is the time between two instances on a timeline.

The usage for a duration as a parsable string is PnDTnHnMnS, where P stands for period and T stands for time. D, H, M, and S are days, hours, minutes, and seconds prefaced by their values (n):

```
Duration d1 = Duration.parse("P2DT3H4M1.1S");
```

Durations can also be created using the of[Type] method. Hours, minutes, seconds, and nanoseconds can be added to their associated status:

```
Duration d2 = Duration.of(41, ChronoUnit.YEARS);

Duration d3 = Duration.ofDays(8);
d3 = d3.plusHours(3);
d3 = d3.plusMinutes(30);
d3 = d3.plusSeconds(55).minusNanos(300);
```

The Duration.between() method can be used to create a Duration from a start and end time:

```
Instant birth =
Instant.parse("1967-09-15T10:30:00Z");
Instant current = Instant.now();
Duration d4 = Duration.between(birth, current);
System.out.print("Days alive: " + d4.toDays());
```

A Period is a date-based amount consisting of years, months, and days.

The usage for a period as a parsable string is PnYnMnD, where P stands for period; Y, M, and D are years, months, and days prefaced by their values (n):

```
Period p1 = Period.parse("P10Y5M2D");
```

Periods can also be created using the of[Type] method. Years, months, and days can be added or subtracted to/from their associated states:

```
Period p2 = Period.of(5, 10, 40);
p2 = p2.plusYears(100);
p2 = p2.plusMonths(5).minusDays(30);
```

## JDBC and XSD Mapping

Interoperation between the java.time and java.sql types has been achieved. Table 18-1 provides a visual mapping of the JSR 310 types to the SQL, as well as XML Schema (XSD) types.

*Table 18-1. JDBC and XSD mapping*

| JSR 310 type | SQL type | XSD type |
| --- | --- | --- |
| LocalDate | DATE | xs:time |
| LocalTime | TIME | xs:time |
| LocalDateTime | TIMESTAMP WITHOUT TIMEZONE | xs:dateTime |
| OffsetTime | TIME WITH TIMEZONE | xs:time |
| OffsetDateTime | TIMESTAMP WITH TIMEZONE | xs:dateTime |
| Period | INTERVAL | . |

## Formatting

The DateTimeFormatter class provides a formatting capability for printing and parsing date-time objects. The upcoming example demonstrates the use of pattern letters with the ofPattern() method of the class. Usable pattern letters are identified in the Javadoc for the DateTimeFormatter class:

```
LocalDateTime input = LocalDateTime.now();
DateTimeFormatter format
  = DateTimeFormatter.ofPattern("yyyyMMddhhmmss");
String date = input.format(format);
String logFile = "simple-log-" + date + ".txt";
```

Table 18-2 contains examples of predefined formatters using the following structure:

```
System.out.print(LocalDateTime.now()
  .format(DateTimeFormatter.BASIC_ISO_DATE));
```

*Table 18-2. Predefined formatters*

| Class | Formatter | Example |
| --- | --- | --- |
| LocalDateTime | BASIC_ISO_DATE | 20140215 |
| LocalDateTime | ISO_LOCAL_DATE | 2014-02-15 |
| OffsetDateTime | ISO_OFFSET_DATE | 2014-02-15-05:00 |
| LocalDateTime | ISO_DATE | 2014-02-15 |
| OffsetDateTime | ISO_DATE | 2014-02-15-05:00 |
| LocalDateTime | ISO_LOCAL_TIME | 23:39:07.884 |
| OffsetTime | ISO_OFFSET_TIME | 23:39:07.888-05:00 |
| LocalDateTime | ISO_TIME | 23:39:07.888 |
| OffsetDateTime | ISO_TIME | 23:39:07.888-05:00 |
| LocalDateTime | ISO_LOCAL_DATE_TIME | 2014-02-15T23:39:07.888 |
| OffsetDateTime | ISO_OFFSET_DATE_TIME | 2014-02-15T23:39:07.888-05:00 |

| Class | Formatter | Example |
|---|---|---|
| ZonedDateTime | ISO_ZONED_DATE_TIME | 2014-02-15T23:39:07.89-05:00 [America/New_York] |
| LocalDateTime | ISO_DATE_TIME | 2014-02-15T23:39:07.891 |
| ZonedDateTime | ISO_DATE_TIME | 2014-02-15T23:39:07.891-05:00 [America/New_York] |
| LocalDateTime | ISO_ORDINAL_DATE | 2014-046 |
| LocalDate | ISO_WEEK_DATE | 2014-W07-6 |
| ZonedDateTime | RFC_1123_DATE_TIME | Sat, 15 Feb 2014 23:39:07 -0500 |

# CHAPTER 19

# Lambda Expressions

Lambda expressions (λEs), also known as *closures*, provide a means to represent anonymous methods. Supported by Project Lambda (*http://openjdk.java.net/projects/lambda/*), λEs allow for the creation and use of single method classes. These methods have a basic syntax that provides for the omission of modifiers, the return type, and optional parameters. The specification for λEs is set out in JSR 335 (*http://bit.ly/JSR-335*), which is divided into seven parts: functional interfaces, lambda expressions, method and constructor references, poly expressions, typing and evaluation, type inference, and default methods. This chapter focuses on the first two.

## λEs Basics

λEs must have a functional interface (FI). An FI is an interface that has one abstract method and zero or more default methods. FIs provide target types for lambda expressions and method references, and ideally should be annotated with @Functional interface to aid the developer and compiler with design intent, as shown in the following code example:

```
@FunctionalInterface
public interface Comparator<T> {
  // Only one abstract method allowed
```

```
  int compare(T o1, T o2);
  // Overriding allowed
  boolean equals(Object obj);
  // Optional default methods allowed
}
```

## λEs Syntax and Example

Lambda expressions typically include a parameter list, a return type, and a body:

```
(parameter list) -> { statements; }
```

Examples of λEs include the following:

```
() -> 66
(x,y) -> x + y
(Integer x, Integer y) -> x*y
(String s) -> { System.out.println(s); }
```

This simple JavaFX GUI application adds text to the title bar when the button is pressed. The code makes use of the EventHandler functional interface with the one abstract method, handle():

```
import javafx.application.Application;
import javafx.event.ActionEvent;
import javafx.event.EventHandler;
import javafx.scene.Scene;
import javafx.scene.control.Button;
import javafx.scene.layout.StackPane;
import javafx.stage.Stage;
public class JavaFxApp extends Application {
  @Override
  public void start(Stage stage) {
    Button b = new Button();
    b.setText("Press Button to Set Title");
    // Anonymous inner class usage
    b.setOnAction(new EventHandler<ActionEvent>() {
      @Override
      public void handle(ActionEvent event) {
        stage.setTitle("λEs rock!");
```

```
      }
    });
    StackPane root = new StackPane();
    root.getChildren().add(b);
    Scene scene = new Scene(root, 300, 100);
    stage.setScene(scene);
    stage.show();
  }
  public static void main(String[] args) {
    launch();
  }
}
```

To refactor this anonymous inner class into a lambda expression, the parameter type needs to be either (ActionEvent event) or just (event), and the desired functionality needs to be provided as statements in the body:

```
// Lambda expression usage
b.setOnAction((ActionEvent event) -> {
  stage.setTitle("λEs rock!");
});
```

---

### TIP

Modern IDEs have features to convert anonymous inner classes to lambda expressions.

---

See "Comparator Functional Interface" on page 158 for another example of lambda expressions with the Comparator functional interface.

## Method and Constructor References

A method reference refers to an existing method without invoking it. Types include static method reference, instance method of particular object, super method of particular object, and instance method of arbitrary object of particular type.

Method references are lambda expressions that execute just one method, as demonstrated in the following examples:

```
"some text"::length  // Get length of String
String::length // Get length of String
CheckAcct::compareByBalance  // Static method ref
myComparator::compareByName // Inst method part obj
super::toString // Super method part object
String::compareToIgnoreCase // Inst method arb obj
ArrayList<String>::new  // New ArrayList construc
tor
Arrays::sort  // Sort array elements
```

## Specific-Purpose Functional Interfaces

Annotated FIs listed in Table 19-1 have been established for specific purposes relative to the packages/APIs in which they reside. Not all functional interfaces in the Java SE API are annotated.

*Table 19-1. Specific-purpose FIs*

| API | Class | Method |
|-----|-------|--------|
| AWT | KeyEventDispacter | dispatchKeyEvent (KeyEvent e) |
| AWT | KeyEventPostProcessor | postProcessKeyEvent (KeyEvent e) |
| IO | FileFilter | accept(File pathname) |
| IO | FilenameFilter | accept(File dir, String name) |
| LANG | Runnable | run () |
| Nashorn | DiagnosticListener | report (Diagnostic diagnostic) |
| NIO | DirectorStream | iterator () |
| NIO | PathMatcher | matches (Path path) |
| TIME | TemporalAdjuster | adjustInto (Temporal temporal) |

| API | Class | Method |
|---|---|---|
| TIME | TemporalQuery | queryFrom (TemporalAccessor temporal) |
| UTIL | Comparator | compare (T o1, T o2) |
| CONC | Callable | call () |
| LOG | Filter | isLoggable (LogRecord record) |
| PREF | PreferenceChangeListener | preferenceChange (PreferenceChangeEvent evt) |

# General-Purpose Functional Interfaces

The java.util.function package is made up of general-purpose FIs for the primary use of features of the JDK. Table 19-2 lists them all.

*Table 19-2. Functional interfaces functional package*

| Class | Method |
|---|---|
| Consumer | accept (T t) |
| BiConsumer | accept (T t, U u) |
| ObjDoubleConsumer | accept (T t, double value) |
| ObjIntConsumer | accept (T t, int value) |
| ObjLongConsumer | accept (T t, long value) |
| DoubleConsumer | accept (double value) |
| IntConsumer | accept (int value) |
| LongConsumer | accept (long value) |
| Function | apply (T t) |
| BiFunction | apply (T t, U u) |
| DoubleFunction | apply (double value) |
| IntFunction | apply (int value) |
| LongFunction | apply (long value) |

| Class | Method |
|---|---|
| BinaryOperator | apply (Object, Object) |
| ToDoubleBiFunction | applyAsDouble (T t, U u) |
| ToDoubleFunction | applyAsDouble (T value) |
| IntToDoubleFunction | applyAsDouble (int value) |
| LongToDoubleFunction | applyAsDouble(long value) |
| DoubleBinaryOperator | applyAsDouble (double left, double right) |
| ToIntBiFunction | applyAsInt (T t, U u) |
| ToIntFunction | applyAsInt (T value) |
| LongToIntFunction | applyAsInt (long value) |
| DoubleToIntFunction | applyAsInt(double value) |
| IntBinaryOperator | applyAsInt (int left, int right) |
| ToLongBiFunction | applyAsLong (T t, U u) |
| ToLongFunction | applyAsLong (T value) |
| DoubleToLongFunction | applyAsLong (double value) |
| IntToLongFunction | applyAsLong (int value) |
| LongBinaryOperator | applyAsLong (long left, long right) |
| BiPredicate | test (T t, U u) |
| Predicate | test (T t) |
| DoublePredicate | test (double value) |
| IntPredicate | test (int value) |
| LongPredicate | test (long value) |
| Supplier | get() |
| BooleanSupplier | getAsBoolean() |
| DoubleSupplier | getAsDouble() |

| Class | Method |
|-------|--------|
| IntSupplier | getAsInt() |
| LongSupplier | getAsLong() |
| UnaryOperator | identity() |
| DoubleUnaryOperator | identity() |
| IntUnaryOperator | applyAsInt (int operand) |
| LongUnaryOperator | applyAsInt (long value) |

# Resources for λEs

This section provides links to tutorials and community resources about λEs.

## Tutorials

Comprehensive tutorials exist, such as those provided by Oracle, O'Reilly Learning, and Maurice Naftalin.

- The Java Tutorials: "Lambda Expressions" (*http://bit.ly/1oHnAAt*)
- "Java 8 functional interfaces" on O'Reilly Learning (*https://www.oreilly.com/learning/java-8-functional-interfaces*)
- Maurice Naftalin's Lambda FAQ: "Your questions answered: all about Lambdas and friends" (*http://www.lambdafaq.org/*)

## Community Resources

Online bulletin boards, mailing lists, and instructional videos provide support for learning and using λEs:

- Java 8's new features (e.g., λEs) forum at CodeRanch (*https://coderanch.com/f/143/java*)

- Oracle Learning Library on YouTube (*http://bit.ly/1m3ZHhs*)

# CHAPTER 20

# JShell: the Java Shell

JShell, originally called *Project Kulla*, is an interactive command-line read-eval-print-loop (REPL) tool introduced in the Java 9 SDK. Similar in functionality to such interpreters as Python's ipython and Haskell's ghci, JShell allows users to evaluate and test fragments of code in real time without the trouble of creating a test project or a class housing a main function.

The code in this chapter was tested against JShell version 9-ea.

## Getting Started

JShell can be launched from the menu of the NetBeans IDE (Tools→Java Platform Shell), from the Windows command line by running jshell.exe from the */bin/* directory of your JDK installation, or in POSIX environments with the jshell command.

When the environment has loaded, you will be greeted with a prompt:

```
|  Welcome to JShell -- Version 9-ea
|  For an introduction type: /help intro


jshell>
```

From here, you will be able to enter, execute, or modify code snippets, or interact with the JShell environment through its built-in commands.

## Snippets

JShell operates upon units called *snippets*, which are code fragments entered by the user at the jshell> prompt. Each snippet must take a form defined in the JLS, as summarized in Table 20-1:

*Table 20-1. Permitted snippet forms*

| Java Language Specification Production | Example |
|---|---|
| Primary | 10 / 2 |
| Statement | if (value == null) { numWidgets = 0; } |
| ClassDeclaration | class Foo { } |
| MethodDeclaration | void sayHello () { Sys tem.out.println("Hello"); } |
| FieldDeclaration | boolean isAnchovyLover = true; |
| InterfaceDeclaration | interface eventHandler { void onThi sEvent(); } |
| ImportDeclaration | import java.math.BigInteger; |

## Modifiers

JShell handles modifiers differently than does standard compiled Java. Most notably, it prohibits the use of several in top-level declarations (i.e., in the main JShell "sandbox" and outside of the scope of a class/method declaration or other nested context). The following example warns the user when the inappropriate use of the private modifier is attempted:

```
jshell> private double airPressure
|  Warning:
```

```
|  Modifier 'private'  not permitted in top-level
   declarations, ignored
|  private double airPressure;
|  ^-----^
airPressure ==> 0.0

jshell> class AirData { private double airPres
sure; }
|  created class AirData
```

Table 20-2 shows a summary of JShell's modifier policies.

*Table 20-2. JShell modifier rules*

| Modifier | Rule |
| --- | --- |
| private, protected, pub lic, final, static | Ignored with warning if top-level declaration |
| abstract, default | Usable only in class declarations |
| default, synchronized | Prohibited in top-level declarations |

## Flow Control Statements

Similarly, the flow control statements break, continue, and return are disallowed at the top level, as they have no relevant meaning in that context.

## Package Declarations

Package declarations are not allowed in JShell, as all JShell code is placed in the transient package jshell.

# Using JShell

As mentioned in "Getting Started" on page 197, your interaction with JShell will primarily consist of entering, manipulating, and executing snippets. The following sections provide detail on working with each of the major snippet varieties, as well as saving and loading code and input histories and restoring and persisting JShell's state.

## Primary Expressions

JShell will immediately evaluate and/or execute any primary expressions entered via the prompt:

```
jshell> 256 / 8
$1 ==> 32

jshell> true || false
$2 ==> true

jshell> 97 % 2
$3 ==> 1

jshell> System.out.println("Hello, Dave. Shall we
continue the game?")
Hello, Dave. Shall we continue the game?

jshell> StringBuilder sb = new StringBuilder("HAL")
sb ==> HAL

jshell> sb.append(" 9000")
$4 ==> HAL 9000
```

Notice that JShell will append missing semicolons to the ends of expressions and statements. Semicolons are, however, required as usual when declaring methods, classes, and other code contained in blocks.

## Dependencies

The command /imports returns a list of all libraries currently imported into the workspace:

```
jshell> /imports
|    import java.io.*
|    import java.math.*
|    import java.net.*
|    import java.nio.file*
|    import java.util.*
|    import java.util.concurrent.*
|    import java.util.function.*
```

```
|    import java.util.prefs.*
|    import java.util.regex.*
|    import java.util.stream.*
```

The results represent the libraries that JShell imports into each new workspace by default. Additional libraries can be imported via the import command:

```
jshell> import java.lang.StringBuilder
```

## Statements and Code Blocks

Like primary expressions, snippets representing statements are immediately executed upon entry:

```
jshell> double[] tempKelvin = {373.16, 200.19, 0.0}
tempKelvin ==> double[3] { 373.16, 200.19, 0.0 }
```

When a statement contains one or more blocks of code, the JShell prompt becomes the new-line prompt (...>) upon the first carriage return press and continues reading the snippet line by line until the highest-level block is terminated:

```
jshell> import java.text.DecimalFormat

jshell> DecimalFormat df = new DecimalFor
mat("#.#");
df ==> java.text.DecimalFormat@674dc

jshell> double[] tempFahrenheit = {30.8, 77.0,
29.3, 60.2 }
tempFahrenheit ==> double[5] { 30.8, 77.0, 29.3,
60.2 }

jshell> for (double temp : tempFahrenheit) {
   ...> double tempCelsius = ((temp - 32)*5/9);
   ...> System.out.println(temp + " degrees F is
equal to "
   ...> + df.format(tempCelsius) + " degrees C.
\n");
   ...> }
30.8 degrees F is equal to -0.7 degrees C.
```

```
77.0 degrees F is equal to 25 degrees C.
29.3 degrees F is equal to -1.5 degrees C.
60.2 degrees F is equal to 15.7 degrees C.
```

If a code block contains a compile-time error such as a syntax error, the snippet will neither be created nor executed and must be re-entered. Although the up arrow key can be used at the prompt to scroll up through previous commands in the line buffer, this still can be a tedious process. Take care, then, to input large code blocks carefully when using the command line.

The command /! can be used to re-execute the snippet that was last run. Similarly, the /-<n> command will execute the prior snippet relative to the number supplied:

```
jshell> System.out.println("Hello");
Hello
jshell> System.out.println("World");
World
jshell> /!
System.out.println("World");
World
jshell> /-3
System.out.println("Hello");
Hello
```

## Method and Class Declarations

Methods are declared in JShell in the same way as any other statements or code blocks, and may be invoked from the command line:

```
jshell> double KELVIN = 273.16
KELVIN ==> 273.16

jshell> double DRY_AIR_GAS_CONSTANT = 287.058
DRY_AIR_GAS_CONSTANT ==> 287.058

jshell> double getDryAirDensity(double temperature,
   ...>    double atmosphericPressure) {
```

```
   ...> // convert from hPa to Pa
   ...> double airDensity = atmosphericPressure *
100
   ...>   / (DRY_AIR_GAS_CONSTANT
   ...>   * (temperature + KELVIN));
   ...> return airDensity;
   ...> }
|  created method getDryAirDensity(double,double)

jshell> double todaysAirDensity =
   ...> getDryAirDensity(15, 1013.25)
todaysAirDensity ==> 1.2249356158607942
```

The command /methods returns a list of all methods currently residing in the workspace, as well as their signatures:

```
jshell> /methods
|     double getDryAirDensity (double,double)
```

The process for declaring classes is the same. In the following example, we wrap the air density calculator code in a utility class to apply the static final modifiers that will make our constants behave as constants:

```
jshell> class AirDensityUtils {
   ...> private static final double KELVIN = 273.16;
   ...> private static final double
   ...>   DRY_AIR_GAS_CONSTANT = 287.058;
   ...>
   ...> double getDryAirDensity(double temperature,
   ...>   double atmosphericPressure) {
   ...> // convert from hPa to Pa
   ...> double airDensity = atmosphericPressure *
100
   ...> / (DRY_AIR_GAS_CONSTANT
   ...> * (temperature + KELVIN));
   ...> return airDensity;
   ...> }
   ...> }
|  created class AirDensityUtils
```

The methods and members of the class can be accessed from the command line via standard Java dot notation. Although Air DensityUtils is a utility class, it cannot be referenced from a static context, as the static modifier is not allowed in top-level declarations, and so must be instantiated:

```
jshell> new AirDensityUtils().
   ...>    getDryAirDensity(15, 1013.25)
$5 ==> 1.2249356158607942
```

Other types, such as interfaces and enums, are also declared this way. The /types command will return a list of all types currently residing in the workspace:

```
jshell> interface EventHandler { void onWeatherDa
taReceived(); }
|  created interface EventHandler

jshell> enum WeatherCondition { RAIN, SNOW, HAIL }
|  created enum WeatherCondition

jshell> /types
|    class AirDenstityUtils
|    interface EventHandler
|    enum WeatherCondition
```

## Viewing, Deleting, and Modifying Snippets

Once they are defined, snippets can be easily viewed, deleted, and modified. The /list command displays a list of all current snippet code, along with corresponding identification numbers:

```
jshell> /list

   1 : double KELVIN = 273.16;
   2 : double DRY_AIR_GAS_CONSTANT = 287.058;
   3 : double getDryAirDensity(double temperature,
        double atmPressure) {
        // convert from hPa to Pa
        double airDensity = atmoPressure * 100
        / (DRY_AIR_GAS_CONSTANT
```

```
        * (temperature + KELVIN));
      return airDensity;
      }
  4 : class AirDensityUtils {
      private static final double
        KELVIN = 273.16;
      private static final double
        DRY_AIR_GAS_CONSTANT = 287.058;

      double getDryAirDensity(double temperature,
        double atmPressure) {
        // convert from hPa to Pa
        double airDensity = atmPressure * 100
        / (DRY_AIR_GAS_CONSTANT *
        (temperature + KELVIN));
        return airDensity;
      }
      }
```

Snippets may be referenced in JShell commands either by name
or by identification number. In the previous example, we made
the two top-level pseudoconstants DRY_AIR_GAS_CONSTANT and
KELVIN superfluous when we wrapped them and getDryAirDen
sity(double, double) in a class, so we will delete them by
using the /drop command:

```
jshell> /drop KELVIN
|  dropped variable KELVIN

jshell> /drop 2
|  dropped variable DRY_AIR_GAS_CONSTANT
```

Modification or replacement of previously defined snippets is
easy, as well. The first method by which to perform this action
is simply to overwrite the original:

```
jshell> double getDryAirDensity(double temperature,
   ...>    double atmPressure) {
   ...>    // We don't need this method anymore,
   ...>    // but let's replace it anyway!
```

```
...> }
```
| `  replaced method getDryAirDensity(double,double)`

This is not a terribly practical solution for cases involving large code fragments or only minor adjustments. Fortunately, JShell also allows snippet code to be modified in an external editor via /edit <name> or /edit <id>.

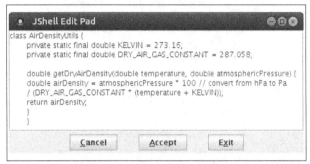

*Figure 20-1. JShell default edit pad*

In Figure 20-1, AirDensityUtils has been opened for editing in the default JShell edit pad. However, the text editor that JShell launches for this task may be specified using /set editor <_command_>, where +*command*+ is the operating system-dependent command to launch one's text editor of choice. For example, in Linux, /set editor vim or /set editor emacs.

Regardless of which method one employs to modify a snippet, any snippets that refer to or depend upon the snippet being modified will not be affected by the change.

## Saving, Loading, and State

The command /save <_file_> will save the source of all current active snippets to the designated filename. Applying the -all flag will save all source code entered during the current session, including overwritten and rejected snippet code; applying the -history flag will save all snippet code and commands in the order in which they were entered.

Conversely, `/open <_file_>` will load the contents of the specified file as JShell input. Be aware that the file will not successfully load if it contains a package declaration.

JShell's state may also be reset or restored while the session is active. The `/reset` command resets JShell's state, clearing all entered code, restarting the execution state, and re-executing any startup code.

The `/reload` command, on the other hand, will reset JShell's code and execution state and replay all valid snippet entries and commands. The replay will commence from the start of the session or from the last `/reset` or `/reload`, whichever happened most recently. Additionally, `/reload -restore` will restore JShell's state from the previous session if used at startup.

JShell can be instructed to load snippets automatically after a `/reset` or `/reload` with the command `/set start <_file_>`, where *file* is a saved collection of snippet code. Further, subsequently using the command `/retain start` will cause the code to load each time JShell starts. This can be a useful feature for those working with the same set of methods and classes from session to session.

# JShell Features

JShell sports a number of conveniences from other shell scripting and interpreter environments, as well as characteristics that set it apart from traditional compiled Java. Notable among these are scratch variables, tab smart-complete, forward referencing, leniency in checked exception handling, and its treatment of top-level variables.

## Scratch Variables

The return value of a stand-alone primary expression or method invocation is stored in a scratch variable, which is prefixed with ($) and which is accessible from within the JShell environment:

```
jshell> 21 + 20
$6 ==> 41

jshell> $6 + 1
$7 ==> 42

jshell> "The meaning of life is " + $7
$8 ==> "The meaning of life is 42"

jshell> $8.getClass().getName()
$9 ==> "java.lang.String"
```

In order to see the return type of a statement without having to invoke getClass(), the user may set JShell's feedback mode to verbose:

```
jshell> /set feedback verbose
|  Feedback mode: verbose

jshell> 7.0 % 2
$10 ==> 1.0
|  created scratch variable $10 : double
```

## Tab Auto-Complete

The JShell environment includes one of the more convenient features of most modern command-line interpreters and shells: tab auto-completion. When the user presses the Tab key, JShell automatically completes partially typed variable, snippet, or object names.

In ambiguous cases, JShell presents the user with a list of possibilities. In the following example, the user presses the Tab key after typing temp, but there are currently three variables in the environment beginning with those characters:

```
shell> temp
tempCelsius        tempFahrenheit     tempKelvin
```

## Forward Referencing

JShell allows for forward referencing in snippet definitions. That is, one may define a method that references other methods, classes, or variables that have not yet been defined. However, any undefined items must be defined before the method may be invoked or referenced:

```
jshell> void getDryAirDensity(
   ...>    MeasurementSystem unit) {
   ...> temperature = x;
   ...> pressure = y;
   ...> adjustUnits(x, y, unit);
   ...> // calculation code
   ...> }
|  created method
getDryAirDensity(MeasurementSystem
), however, it cannot be referenced until
class Measure mentSystem, variable
temperature, variable pressure, and
variable y are declared
```

Undefined classes may not be used as return types in method declarations, nor may any members, methods, or constructors of undefined classes be referenced.

## Checked Exceptions

If a a single, stand-alone statement invokes a method that throws a checked exception, JShell will automatically provide the exception handling behind the scenes without any additional input from the user:

```
jshell> BufferedReader bReader = new Buffere
dReader(
   ...>    new FileReader("message.txt"))
bReader ==> java.io.BufferedReader@1e3c938

jshell> String txtLine;
txtLine ==> null
```

```
jshell> while ((txtLine = bReader.readLine()) !=
null)
   ...> { System.out.println(txtLine); }
I don't like macaroni cheese.  And I don't like
scrambled eggs.  And I don't like cocoa.

jshell> bReader.close()
```

In the preceding example, three file I/O operations are success-fully performed without any IOException handling. However, when a snippet is a method or class declaration (i.e., it does not constitute one single, discrete statement), its code must handle any thrown exceptions as usual:

```
jshell> void displayMessage() {
   ...> BufferedReader bReader = new Buffere
dReader(
   ...>   new FileReader("message.txt"));
   ...> String txtLine;
   ...> while ((txtLine = bReader.readLine()) !=
null)
   ...>   { System.out.println(txtLine); }
   ...> bReader.close();
   ...> }
|  Error:
|  unreported exception java.io.FileNotFoundExcep
tion; must be caught or declared to be thrown
|  BufferedReader bReader = new BufferedReader(new
FileReader("message.txt"));
|
|  Error:
|  unreported exception java.io.IOException; must
be caught or declared to be thrown
|  while ((textLine = bReader.readLine()) != null)
{ System.out.println(textLine); }
|
|  Error:
|  unreported exception java.io.IOException; must
be caught or declared to be thrown
|  bReader.close();
|
```

## Hierarchy and Scope

An interesting feature of the JShell environment is that variables, methods, and classes declared at the top level are accessible from any scope in the JShell hierarchy.

This is due to the fact that the JShell interpreter wraps snippets within a synthetic class in order to make them comprehensible to the Java compiler, which only recognizes import statements and class declarations at the top level.

Specifically, top-level JShell variable, method, and class declarations are made static members of this synthetic class, while statements and primary expressions are enclosed in synthetic methods and then added to it. Import statements, being a recognized top-level construct, are placed unmodified at the top of the synthetic class.

The following example's method and class both read and modify the top-level `double` variable `pressure` from within their respective scopes:

```
jshell> double pressure = 30.47
pressure ==> 30.47

jshell> void convertPressureinHgTohPa() {
   ...> pressure = pressure * 33.86389;
   ...> }
|  created method convertPressureinHgTohPa()

jshell> convertPressureinHgTohPa()

jshell> pressure
pressure ==> 1031.8327282999999

jshell> class WeatherStation {
   ...> double mAirPressure;
   ...> public WeatherStation() {
   ...> mAirPressure = pressure;
   ...> }
   ...> }
```

```
|  created class WeatherStation

jshell> WeatherStation ws = new WeatherStation()
ws ==> WeatherStation@b1ffe6

jshell> ws.mAirPressure
$11 ==> 1031.8327282999999
```

Such an example is not likely to win any accolades for programming best practices, but as JShell is an excellent playground for experimentation and quick, informal code testing, some may find this quirk useful.

## Summary of JShell Commands

Table 20-3 shows a list of all commands available in the JShell environment. It may be accessed at any time from within JShell via the /help command.

*Table 20-3. JShell commands*

| Command | Description |
|---------|-------------|
| /list [<name or id>|-all|-start] | Lists source code entered into JShell |
| /edit <name or id> | Edits source entry corresponding with name or ID |
| /drop <name or id> | Deletes source entry corresponding with name or ID |
| /save [-all|-history|-start] <file> | Saves specified snippets and/or commands to file |
| /open <file> | Opens file as source input |
| /vars [<name or id>|-all|-start] | Lists declared variables and corresponding values |
| /methods [<name or id>|-all|-start] | Lists declared methods and corresponding signatures |

| Command | Description |
| --- | --- |
| /types [<name or id>\|-all\|-start] | Lists declared classes, interfaces, and enums |
| /imports | Lists current active JShell imports |
| /exit | Exit JShell without saving |
| /reset | Resets JShell's state |
| /reload [-restore] [-quiet] | Resets JShell state and replays history since JShell start or most recent /reset or /reload command |
| /history | Displays history of all snippets and commands entered since JShell was started |
| /help [<command>\| <subject>] | Displays list of JShell commands and help subjects or further information on specified command or subject |
| /set editor\|start\| feedback\|mode\| prompt\|truncation\| format | Sets JShell configuration options |
| /retain editor\| start\|feedback\|mode | Retains settings for use in subsequent JShell sessions |
| /? [<command>\|<sub ject>] | Identical to /help |
| /! | Re-runs last snippet |
| /<id> | Re-runs a snippet referenced by ID |
| /-<n> | Re-runs nth previous snippet |

# CHAPTER 21

# Java Module System

Java 9 introduces the Project Jigsaw, which both adds modularization to the platform and modularizes the JDK itself. The goal of Jigsaw is twofold: to enable reliable configuration and add strong encapsulation to Java. With modularization, it is now possible to restrict which packages are public and also ensure that runtime dependencies are present when an application is launched.

The Java Platform Module System (JPMS) is implemented as a separate layer within the JVM. This distinguishes it from other module systems, such as OSGi, which implemented using Classloaders. JPMS enables modularization of the JDK itself.

## Project Jigsaw

Project Jigsaw is made up of a JSR (Java Specification Request) and multiple JEPs (JDK Enhancement Proposals). The specifications that make up Jigsaw are as follows:

- JSR 376 Java Platform Module System
- JEP 200: Modular JDK
- JEP 201: Modular Source Code
- JEP 220: Modular Runtime Images

- JEP 260: Encapsulate Most Internal APIs
- JEP 261: Module System
- JEP 282: jlink: Java Linker

The main project page (*http://openjdk.java.net/projects/jigsaw/*) for Jigsaw has links to each of these specifications.

# Java Modules

Java modules are a JAR file containing a `module-info.java` file in the default package. Since "module-info" is an invalid Java class name, it is ignored by Java 8 and earlier. It does get compiled to bytecode and is available via reflection. The module file declares the name of the module, dependencies of a module, and which packages are exported by this module. Services provided by this module can also be specified in this file.

The module system has the following rules:

- Modules specify which packages are exported. Public types within these packages are available to other modules.
- Packages not exported are not accessible and Java reflection cannot be used to access types at runtime.
- Module names must be globally unique. Reverse domain names should be used as the module name.
- Only one version of a module may be loaded. Multiple versions can be loaded using layers (see `java.lang.ModuleLayer`).
- Module dependency graph cannot contain cycles.
- All modules' dependencies must be present on startup. Any missing dependencies result in an error.
- Module path, analogous to the classpath, has been added to Java tools.

Java applications do not need to be modularized to run on Java 9. If the code is loaded using the classpath instead of the module path, the code will run as it did pre-Java 9. If code is loaded using the module path, then the module graph is resolved and dependencies are checked.

With a JAR file, how it is interpreted by the module system is dependent upon whether it is loaded on the module path or classpath and also whether it contains a `module-info.java` file. JPMS will create either an application module, unnamed module, or automatic module. Table 21-1 gives the breakdown of the behavior.

*Table 21-1. JPMS loading behavior*

|                 | --module-path      | -classpath      |
| --------------- | ------------------ | --------------- |
| Modular JAR     | Application module | Unnamed module  |
| Nonmodular JAR  | Automatic module   | Unnamed module  |

## Automatic Modules

JPMS will automatically create a module for JAR files added to the module path which are missing `module-info.java`. All packages in an automatic module are exported. The name of the automatic module is derived from the name of the JAR file. The rules for the module name are as follows:

- ".jar" suffix is removed.
- The module name will be extracted from the text preceding the hyphen of the first occurrence of the regular expressions `-(\\d(\\.|$))+`, and the version will be extracted after the hyphen if it can be parsed.
- All nonalphanumeric characters will be replaced with a dot, all repeating dots are replaced by a single dot, and all leading/trailing dots are removed.

Table 21-2 shows some examples of module names.

*Table 21-2. Module name examples*

| JAR name | Module name | Version |
|----------|-------------|---------|
| forex-calc.jar | forex.calc | None |
| forex-calc-0.1.0.jar | forex.calc | 0.1.0 |
| forex-0.1.0.jar | forex | 0.1.0 |

## Unnamed Modules

Classes loaded from the classpath, as opposed to the module path, are loaded as an unnamed module. Classes in the unnamed module are not visible to classes on the module path.

## Accessibility

Modules add a new layer of encapsulation to Java. With modules, it is possible to restrict access to public types and selectively declare which modules can access a package. A public class is no longer globally public. A public class can be limited to just its module, or it can be exported and publically accessible to other modules.

# Compiling Modules

The `javac` compiler command has been extended with additional parameters for handling modules. Multiple modules may be compiled simultaneously. For multiple modules, each module's content should be placed in a directory with the same name of the module. An example of this is shown in Figure 21-1.

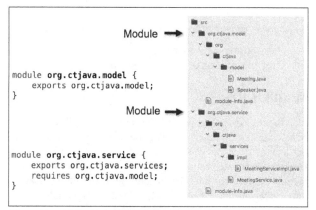

```
module org.ctjava.model {
    exports org.ctjava.model;
}
```

```
module org.ctjava.service {
    exports org.ctjava.services;
    requires org.ctjava.model;
}
```

*Figure 21-1. Multiple-module layout example*

The example in Figure 21-1 would be compiled with the following command line on a Unix system:

```
javac -d out --module-source-path src $(find .
  -name "*.java")
```

Other module command-line options:

`--add-modules <module>(,<module>)*`
Root modules to resolve in addition to the initial modules, or all modules on the module path if <module> is ALL-MODULE-PATH

`--limit-modules <module>(,<module>)*`
Limit the universe of observable modules

`--module <module-name>, -m <module-name>`
Compile only the specified module, check timestamps

`--module-path <path>, -p <path>`
Specify where to find application modules

`--module-source-path <module-source-path>`
Specify where to find input source files for multiple modules

```
--module-version <version>
```
Specify version of modules that are being compiled

```
--upgrade-module-path <path>
```
Override location of upgradeable modules

# Modular JDK

As a part of Project Jigsaw (JEP 200), the JDK itself was heavily refactored and modularized. The module `java.base` is present by default, meaning you do not need to explicitly require it. However, if you are using JavaFX, JDBC, etc., you will need to include the relevant modules in addition to adding the relevant imports to your code. See Table 21-3 for a list of modules.

The Java compiler uses the `java.se.ee` module, whereas at runtime Java uses the `java.se` module. The functionality contained in `java.se.ee` is typically provided by a Java EE container.

*Table 21-3. Module summary*

| Module | Requires |
| --- | --- |
| java.activation | java.base, java.datatransfer, java.logging |
| java.base | |
| java.compiler | java.base |
| java.cobra | java.base, java.desktop, java.logging, java.naming, java.rmi, java.transaction, jdk.unsupported <br> + 4 transitive dependencies |
| java.datatransfer | java.base |
| java.desktop | java.base, java.datatransfer, java.prefs, java.xml |
| java.instrument | java.base |
| java.logging | java.base |
| java.management | java.base |
| java.management.rmi | java.base, java.management, java.naming, java.rmi <br> + 2 transitive dependencies |

| Module | Requires |
|---|---|
| java.naming | java.base, java.security.sasl<br>+ 1 transitive dependency |
| java.prefs | java.base, java.xml |
| java.rmi | java.base, java.logging |
| java.scripting | java.base |
| java.se | java.base, java.compiler, java.datatransfer,<br>java.desktop, java.instrument, java.logging,<br>java.management, java.management.rmi,<br>java.naming, java.prefs, java.rmi, java.scripting,<br>java.security.jgss, java.security.sasl, java.sql,<br>java.sql.rowset, java.xml, java.xml.crypto |
| java.se.ee | java.activation, java.base, java.corba, java.se,<br>java.transaction, java.xml.bind, java.xml.ws,<br>java.xml.ws.annotation<br>+ 19 transitive dependencies |
| java.security.jgss | java.base, java.naming<br>+ 2 transitive dependencies |
| java.security.sasl | java.base, java.logging |
| java.smartcardio | java.base |
| java.sql | java.base, java.logging, java.xml |
| java.sql.rowset | java.base, java.logging, java.naming, java.sql<br>+ 2 transitive dependencies |
| java.transaction | java.base,java.rmi<br>+ 1 transitive dependency |
| java.xml | java.base |
| java.xml.bind | java.activation, java.base, java.compiler, java.desktop,<br>java.logging, java.xml, jdk.unsupported<br>+ 2 transitive dependencies |
| java.xml.crypto | java.base, java.logging, java.xml |

| Module | Requires |
|---|---|
| java.xml.ws | java.activation, java.base, java.desktop, java.logging, java.management, java.xml, java.xml.bind, java.xml.ws.annotation, jdk.httpserver, jdk.unsupported<br>+ 3 transitive dependencies |
| java.xml.ws.annotation | java.base |

# jdeps

To prepare for Project Jigsaw in Java 9, Oracle added the jdeps command-line tool in Java 8. This is a static dependency checker, which is meant to aid in preparation for Java 9. This tool has three primary uses:

- Identify which JDK modules are required for a set of classes.

- Trace transitive dependencies of a set of classes.

- Identify dependencies on undocumented internal JDK classes.

The utility can generate the analysis on the console or dump it to a .dot file. Tools such as graphviz (*https://graphviz.org*) can use the .dot file to render the output graphically.

## Identifying Dependencies

```
jdeps postgresql-42.1.1.jar

    postgresql-42.1.1.jar -> /Library/Java/JavaVirtual
    Machines/jdk1.8.0_131.jdk/Contents/Home/jre/lib/
    jce.jar
    postgresql-42.1.1.jar -> not found
    postgresql-42.1.1.jar -> /Library/Java/JavaVirtual
    Machines/jdk1.8.0_131.jdk/Contents/Home/jre/lib/
    rt.jar
     org.postgresql (postgresql-42.1.1.jar)
     -> java.io
```

```
-> java.lang
-> java.net
-> java.security
-> java.sql
-> java.util
-> java.util.logging
-> org.postgresql.copy postgresql-42.1.1.jar
-> org.postgresql.fastpath postgresql-42.1.1.jar
-> org.postgresql.jdbc postgresql-42.1.1.jar
-> org.postgresql.largeobject
postgresql-42.1.1.jar
-> org.postgresql.replication
postgresql-42.1.1.jar
-> org.postgresql.util postgresql-42.1.1.jar
...
```

## Identifying Undocumented JDK Internal Dependencies

To identify dependencies on undocumented JDK classes, use
-jdkinternals. Undocumented JDK classes are those that
begin with com.sun.* or sun.*. These were not meant to be
used outside of the JDK and may be removed at any point.
With Java 9, many of these APIs have been refactored or
removed.

The following jdeps command invocation returns the dependencies for the MyEncoder jar:

```
jdeps -jdkinternals MyEncoder.jar

    MyEncoder.jar -> /Library/Java/JavaVirtualMachines/
    jdk1.8.0_131.jdk/Contents/Home/jre/lib/rt.jar
     org.ctjava.util.TransmitUtil (MyEncoder.jar)
     -> sun.misc.BASE64Encoder JDK internal API
    (rt.jar)

    Warning: JDK internal APIs are unsupported and pri
    vate to JDK implementation that are
    subject to be removed or changed incompatibly and
    could break your application.
```

```
Please modify your code to eliminate dependency on
any JDK internal APIs.
For the most recent update on JDK internal API
replacements, please check:
https://wiki.openjdk.java.net/display/JDK8/Java
+Dependency+Analysis+Tool

JDK Internal API Suggested Replacement
---------------- ---------------------
sun.misc.BASE64Encoder Use java.util.Base64 @since
1.8
```

In this example, the class TransmitUtil depends upon an undocumented JDK class which isn't supported in Java 9.

## Defining a Module

To define a module, a module-info.java file must be created in
the default package. The content of the file is as follows:

```
<open> module <module-name> {
        [export <java package> [to <module name>]
   [requires [transitive] [static] <module-name>]
   [opens <module name> [to <module name]]
        [provides <interface> with <implementa
tion>]
        [uses <interface>]
}
```

The module name must be unique and should use the reverse
domain name pattern. The following example defines module
with the name org.ctjava.admin, which doesn't export any
packages or depend upon any modules:

```
module org.ctjava.admin {
}
```

## Exporting a Package

All public types in a package may be exported by adding one or
more export statements to the module definition:

---

```
module org.ctjava.admin {
  exports org.ctjava.admin.api
}
```

In this example, all public classes in org.ctjava.admin.api are exported and available to other modules that depend upon org.ctjava.admin.

Packages can be selectively exported to a specific module, for example:

```
module org.ctjava.admin {
  exports org.ctjava.admin.ui to javafx.graphics;
}
```

In this example, org.ctjava.admin.ui is selectively exported to javafx.graphics. This gives classes in javafx.graphics access to classes within org.ctjava.admin.ui without this packaging having to declare a dependency in its module file. This is typically done when another package uses reflection. Without the export, classes in javafx.graphics would not be able to perform reflection on classes in org.ctjava.admin.ui.

## Declaring Dependencies

To declare a dependency upon another package, add the requires statement to the module definition. The following example has three dependencies, which must be present when the module is loaded at runtime:

```
module org.ctjava.admin {
    requires javafx.controls;
    requires org.ctjava.services;
    requires org.ctjava.message.api;
}
```

The optional static keyword is for compile time dependencies.

# Transitive Dependencies

If a module is exporting a package which uses classes from another module and which will be required by downstream dependencies, then the dependency must include the `transitive` keyword.

Consider the following module definition:

```
module org.ctjava.services {
    requires transitive org.ctjava.model;
    exports org.ctjava.services;
}
```

This definition will export the org.ctjava.services package, which contains the following class:

```
public interface MeetingService {
    void scheduleMeeting(Meeting meeting,
            Date scheduledDate);
    void updateMeeting(Meeting meeting);
    ...
    }
}
```

This class uses the type Meeting from the org.ctjava.model package. If org.ctjava.services didn't include the transitive keyword on the requires for org.ctjava.model, then users who depend upon org.ctjava.services would not have access to the Meeting class and hence could not invoke/use the Meeting Service class.

# Defining Service Providers

Modules can be defined that export a service which can be dynamically added to the module path on startup. The Service Provider API was first added in Java 6 and has been modified for Java 9. With Service Providers, you have the following:

- A module containing interfaces for a service

- One or more modules containing the implementation of the service
- A module that uses the service

Figure 21-1 shows an example service implementation. The modules are as follows:

org.ctjava.message.api::Contains an interface MessageService.java org.ctjava.email::Contains an implementation of MessageService.java org.ctjava.admin::Uses implementations of org.ctjava.message.api added to the module path.

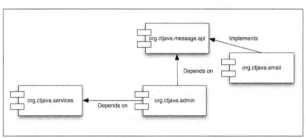

*Figure 21-2. Service Provider API example*

## Defining Service API

The module org.ctjava.message.api, contains MessageService.java defining the contract for the service:

```
module org.ctjava.message.api {
    exports org.ctjava.message.api;
}
```

The package org.ctjava.message.api contains an interface defining the service:

```
package org.ctjava.message.api;

public interface MessageService {
    void sendMessage(String memeber, String message);
}
```

## Implementing Service API

Providing an implementation of a service is straightforward. The module file declares a dependency on service API and specifies that it provides an implementation of the interface. The new `requires` and `provides` keywords are needed in the relative statements to declare the dependency as shown here:

```
module org.ctjava.email {
    requires org.ctjava.message.api;
    provides org.ctjava.message.api.MessageService
            with org.ctjava.email.EmailMessageSer
vice;
}
```

The implementation of the service is straightforward:

```
package org.ctjava.email;

import org.ctjava.message.api.MessageService;

public class EmailMessageService implements Message
Service {
    @Override
    public void sendMessage(String memeber, String
message) {
        // send message
    }
}
```

## Using Service Providers

To use a service, a dependency upon the API is declared, along with a `uses` statement specifying the interface of the service, as shown here:

```
module org.ctjava.admin {
    requires org.ctjava.message.api;
    uses org.ctjava.message.api.MessageService;
}
```

To use the service, use `java.util.ServiceLoader` to get a reference:

```
Iterable<MessageService> mservice = Service
Loader.load(MessageService.class);
for(MessageService ms : mservice) {
  ms.sendMessage(member, "Hello World!");
}
```

# jlink

The jlink tool assembles and optimizes a set of modules and their dependencies into a custom runtime image. This utility is defined in JEP 282. Only required modules are included in the image. For example, a desktop application using JavaFX is only 95 MB versus 454 MB for the full JDK.

The command `jlink` has the following parameters:

```
jlink --module-path <modulepath> +
      --add-modules <modules> +
      --limit-modules <modules> +
      --output <path>
```

Here's an example:

```
jlink --module-path $JAVA_HOME/jmods:dist --add-modules
org.ctjava.TimerUtil --output test
```

# PART III
# Appendixes

# Fluent APIs

Fluent APIs, a.k.a. fluent interfaces, are object-oriented APIs designed to make the API code more readable and therefore easier to use. Wiring objects together via method chaining helps accomplish these readability and usability goals. In this design and the following example, chained methods generally maintain the same type.

```
/*
 * Transform 'palindrome!' string
 * to 'semordnilap' string.
 */

// StringBuilder API
StringBuilder sb = new StringBuilder("palin
drome!");

// Method chaining (delete, append, reverse)
sb.delete(10, 11).append("s").reverse();

System.out.println("New value: " + sb);
$ New value: semordnilap
```

To name a few popular fluent APIs written in Java, there is the Java Object Oriented Querying (jOOQ) API, the jMock testing

API, the Calculon Android testing API, the Apache Camel integration patterns API, Java 8's Date Time API (JSR 310), and the Java Money and Currency API (JSR 354). Each of these is considered to contain a Java domain-specific language (DSL).

An external DSL can be easily mapped into a new Java internal DSL by using the fluent API approach.

Common method prefixes used in fluent APIs include at, for mat, from, get, to, and with.

The LocalDateTime class of the Date Time API is represented here, with and without method chaining:

```java
// Static method with method chaining
LocalDateTime ldt2 = LocalDateTime.now()
  .withDayOfMonth(1).withYear(1878)
  .plusWeeks(2).minus(3, ChronoUnit.HOURS);
System.out.println(ldt2);

$ 1878-02-15T06:33:25.724

// Standalone static method without method chaining
LocalDateTime ldt1 = LocalDateTime.now();
System.out.println(ldt1);

$ 2016-11-06T16:10:12.344
```

---

**TIP**

Consider reviewing *Domain Specific Languages* by Martin Fowler (Addison-Wesley) for comprehensive information on DSLs.

---

# Third-Party Tools

A wide variety of open source and commercial third-party tools and technologies are available to assist you with developing Java-based applications.

The sample set of resources listed here are both effective and popular, or at least many that we have used frequently. Remember to check the licensing agreements of the open source tools you are using for commercial environment restrictions.

## Development, CM, and Test Tools

*Ant (http://bit.ly/16mhLiI)*
> Apache Ant is an XML-based tool for building and deploying Java applications. It's similar to the well-known Unix *make* utility.

*Bloodhound (http://bit.ly/1i4Qkfw)*
> Apache Bloodhound is an open source web-based project management and bug tracking system.

*CruiseControl (http://bit.ly/16mhM6j)*
> CruiseControl is a framework for a continuous build process.

*Enterprise Architect (http://bit.ly/16mhNqN)*

Enterprise Architect is a commercial computer-aided software engineering (CASE) tool that provides forward and reverse Java code engineering with UML.

*FindBugs (http://bit.ly/16mhMTO)*

FindBugs is a program that looks for bugs in Java code.

*Git (http://bit.ly/16mhOep)*

Git is an open source distributed version control system.

*Gradle (http://bit.ly/1eTp2Xs)*

Gradle is a build system that provides testing, publishing, and deployment support.

*Hudson (http://bit.ly/16mhPii)*

Hudson is an extensible continuous integration server.

*Ivy (https://ant.apache.org/ivy/)*

Apache Ivy is a transitive relation dependency manager. It is integrated with Apache Ant.

*Javacc (https://javacc.org/)*

Javacc is a tool that reads a grammar specification and converts it to a Java application that can recognize grammar matches.

*Jalopy (http://bit.ly/16mhRGY)*

Jalopy is a source code formatter for Java that has plug-ins for Eclipse, jEdit, NetBeans, and other tools.

*jClarity (http://www.jclarity.com)*

jClarity is a performance analysis and monitoring tool for cloud environments.

*jEdit (http://bit.ly/16mhTi5)*

jEdit is a text editor designed for programmers. It has several plug-ins available through a plug-in manager.

*JavaFX SceneBuilder (http://bit.ly/2fKFvp9)*

JavaFX Scene Builder is a visual layout tool for designing JavaFX applications.

*Jenkins (http://bit.ly/XUeClg)*

Jenkins CI is an open source continuous integration server, formally known as *Hudson Labs*.

*JIRA (http://bit.ly/16mhVGM)*

JIRA is a commercial bug tracking, issue tracking, and project management application.

*JUnit (http://bit.ly/16mhWdY)*

JUnit is a framework for unit testing that provides a means to write and run repeatable tests.

*JMeter (http://bit.ly/16mhUCH)*

Apache JMeter is an application that measures system behavior, such as functional behavior and performance.

*Maven (http://bit.ly/16mhV9O)*

Apache Maven is a software project management tool. Maven can manage builds, reports, and documentation.

*Nemo (http://bit.ly/16mhYm2)*

Nemo is an online instance of Sonar dedicated to open source projects.

*PMD (http://bit.ly/16mhY5z)*

PMD scans Java source code for bugs, suboptimal code, and overly complicated expressions.

*SonarQube (http://bit.ly/16mhZ9B)*

SonarQube is an open source quality management platform.

*Subversion (http://bit.ly/16mhZq9)*

Apache Subversion is a centralized version control system that keeps track of work and changes for a set of files.

# Libraries

*ActiveMQ (http://bit.ly/16mhZWY)*

Apache ActiveMQ is a message broker that supports many cross-language clients and protocols.

*BIRT (http://bit.ly/16mi0dz)*

    BIRT is an open source Eclipse-based reporting system to be used with Java EE applications.

*Bitlyj (https://github.com/criedel/bitlyj)*

    A DSL for Bitly-powered URL shortening services.

*Camel (http://bit.ly/1ijRVyI)*

    Apache Camel is a rule-based routing and mediation engine.

*gedcom4j (http://gedcom4j.org/main/)*

    gedcom4j is a Java library for parsing, manipulating, and writing GEDCOM data.

*Geocoder-java (https://github.com/panchmp/geocoder-java)*

    Geocoder-java is a Java API for Google geocoder v3.

*GSON (https://github.com/google/gson)*

    Google-gson is a Java API that can convert Java Objects into JSON and back.

*Guava (https://github.com/google/guava)*

    Google Guava is a set of libraries that includes new collection types, immutable collections, a graph library, functional types, an in-memory cache, concurrency utilities, I/O, hashing, primitives and reflection.

*Hibernate (http://bit.ly/16mi2Ck)*

    Hibernate is an object/relational persistence and query service. It allows for the development of persistent classes.

*iText (http://bit.ly/16mi3Gp)*

    iText is a Java library that allows for the creation and manipulation of PDF documents.

*Jakarta Commons (http://bit.ly/16mi4tM)*

    Jakarta Commons is a repository of reusable Java components.

*Jackrabbit (http://bit.ly/16mi4da)*

    Apache Jackrabbit is a content repository system that provides hierarchical content storage and control.

*JasperReports (http://bit.ly/16mi6Sy)*
  JasperReports is an open source Java reporting engine.

*Jasypt (http://bit.ly/16mi796)*
  Jasypt is a Java library that allows the developer to add basic encryption capabilities.

*JFreeChart (http://bit.ly/16mi5hq)*
  JFreeChart is a Java class library for generating charts.

*JFXtras2 (http://bit.ly/16mi5Oy)*
  JFXtras2 is a set of controls and add-ons for JavaFX 2.0.

*JGoodies (http://bit.ly/16mi90J)*
  JGoodies provides components and solutions to solve common user interface tasks.

*JIDE (http://bit.ly/16mi5Oh)*
  JIDE software provides various Java and Swing components.

*jMonkeyEngine (http://jmonkeyengine.org/)*
  jMonkeyEngine is a collection of libraries providing a Java 3D (OpenGL) game engine.

*JOGL (https://jogamp.org/jogl/www/)*
  JOGL is a Java API supporting OpenGL and ES specifications.

*jOOQ (http://www.jooq.org/)*
  jOOQ is a fluent API for typesafe SQL query construction and execution.

*Moneta (http://javamoney.github.io/ri.html)*
  Moneta is a reference implementation of the JSR 354 Money & Currency API.

*opencsv (http://opencsv.sourceforge.net/)*
  opencsv is a comma-separated values (CSV) parser library for Java.

*POI (http://bit.ly/LBob50)*
> Apache Poor Obfuscation Implementation (POI) is a library for reading and writing Microsoft Office formats.

*ROME (https://rometools.github.io/rome/)*
> ROME is a Java framework for RSS and Atom feeds.

*RXTX (http://bit.ly/16mid0f)*
> RXTX provides native serial and parallel communications for Java.

*Spring (http://bit.ly/16midgS)*
> Spring is a layered Java/Java EE application framework.

*Tess4J (http://tess4j.sourceforge.net/)*
> A Java JNA wrapper for the Tesseract optical character recognition (OCR) API.

*Twitter4j (http://twitter4j.org/en/index.html/)*
> A Java library for the Twitter API.

# Integrated Development Environments

*BlueJ (http://bit.ly/16migJu)*
> BlueJ is an IDE designed for introductory teaching.

*Eclipse IDE (http://bit.ly/16mih05)*
> Eclipse IDE is an open source IDE for creating desktop, mobile, and web applications.

*Greenfoot (http://bit.ly/1ef1kIv)*
> Greenfoot is a simple IDE designed to teach object orientation with Java.

*IntelliJ IDEA (http://bit.ly/16miel3)*
> IntelliJ IDEA is a commercial IDE for creating desktop, mobile, and web applications.

*JCreator (http://bit.ly/16mihNJ)*
> JCreator is a commercial IDE for creating desktop, mobile, and web applications.

*JDeveloper (http://bit.ly/15XCBkv)*
> JDeveloper is Oracle's IDE for creating desktop, mobile, and web applications.

*NetBeans IDE (http://bit.ly/16miikG)*
> NetBeans is Oracle's open source IDE for creating desktop, mobile, and web applications. This IDE is currently in the Apache Incubator.

# Web Application Platforms

*Geronimo (http://bit.ly/16miiBc)*
> Apache Geronimo is a Java EE server used for applications, portals, and web services.

*Glassfish (http://bit.ly/16migcz)*
> Glassfish is an open source Java EE server used for applications, portals, and web services. Payara is a GlassFish derivative.

*IBM WebSphere (http://ibm.co/16mij8l)*
> IBM WebSphere is a commercial Java EE server used for applications, portals, and web services.

*JavaServer Faces (https://jcp.org/en/jsr/detail?id=314)*
> JavaServer Faces technology simplifies building user interfaces for Java server applications. JSF implementations and component sets include Apache MyFaces, ICEFaces, RichFaces, and Primefaces.

*Jetty (http://bit.ly/16miksP)*
> Jetty is a web container for Java Servlets and JavaServer Pages.

*Oracle WebLogic Application Server (http://bit.ly/16mikZM)*
> Oracle WebLogic Application Server is a commercial Java EE server used for applications, portals, and web services.

*Resin (http://bit.ly/16milgv)*
> Resin is a high-performance, cloud-optimized Java application server.

*ServiceMix (http://servicemix.apache.org/)*

Apache ServiceMix is an enterprise service bus that combines the functionality of a service-oriented architecture and an event-driven architecture on the Java Business Integration specification.

*Sling (http://bit.ly/16mioZF)*

Sling is a web application framework that leverages the Representational State Transfer (REST) software architecture style.

*Struts (http://bit.ly/16mipwx)*

Apache Struts is a framework for creating enterprise-ready Java web applications that utilize a model-view-controller architecture.

*Tapestry (http://bit.ly/16miq3x)*

Apache Tapestry is a framework for creating web applications based upon the Java Servlet API.

*Tomcat (http://bit.ly/16misIJ)*

Apache Tomcat is a web container for Java Servlets and JavaServer Pages.

*TomEE (http://tomee.apache.org/)*

Apache TomEE is an all-Apache Java EE 6 Web Profile certified stack.

*WildFly (http://www.wildfly.org/)*

WildFly, formally known as *JBoss Application Server*, is an open source Java EE server used for applications, portals, and web services.

# Scripting Languages Compatible with JSR-223

*BeanShell (http://bit.ly/16mitfM)*

BeanShell is an embeddable Java source interpreter with object-based scripting language features.

*Clojure (http://bit.ly/16miwIo)*

Clojure is a dynamic programming language targeted for the Java Virtual Machine, Common Language Runtime, and JavaScript engines.

*FreeMarker (http://bit.ly/16miwZa)*

FreeMarker is a Java-based general-purpose template engine.

*Groovy (http://www.groovy-lang.org/)*

Groovy is a scripting language with many Python, Ruby, and Smalltalk features in a Java-like syntax.

*Jacl (http://bit.ly/16miws2)*

Jacl is a pure Java implementation of the Tcl scripting language.

*JEP (http://bit.ly/16mixMz)*

Java Math Expression Parser (JEP) is a Java library for parsing and evaluating mathematical expressions.

*Jawk (http://bit.ly/16miz7h)*

Jawk is a pure Java implementation of the AWK scripting language.

*Jelly (http://bit.ly/16miD6O)*

Jelly is a scripting tool used for turning XML into executable code.

*JRuby (http://bit.ly/16miEHY)*

JRuby is a pure Java implementation of the Ruby programming language.

*Jython (http://bit.ly/16miG2B)*

Jython is a pure Java implementation of the Python programming language.

*Nashorn (http://bit.ly/1komFPD)*

Nashorn is a JavaScript implementation. It is the *only* scripting language that has a script engine implementation included in the Java Scripting API by default.

*Scala (http://bit.ly/16miGQf)*

Scala is a general-purpose programming language designed to express common programming patterns in a concise, elegant, and type-safe way.

*Sleep (http://bit.ly/16miIY9)*

Sleep, based on Perl, is an embeddable scripting language for Java applications.

*Velocity (http://bit.ly/16miKzh)*

Apache Velocity is a Java-based general-purpose template engine.

*Visage (http://code.google.com/p/visage/)*

Visage is a domain-specific language (DSL) designed for the express purpose of writing user interfaces.

# UML Basics

Unified Modeling Language (UML) is an object-modeling specification language that uses graphical notation to create an abstract model of a system. The Object Management Group (*http://bit.ly/16miJLR*) governs UML. This modeling language can be applied to Java programs to help graphically depict such things as class relationships and sequence diagrams. The latest specifications for UML can be found at the OMG website (*http://bit.ly/16miLmZ*). An informative book on UML is *UML Distilled*, Third Edition, by Martin Fowler (Addison-Wesley).

## Class Diagrams

A class diagram represents the static structure of a system, displaying information about classes and the relationships between them. The individual class diagram is divided into three compartments: name, attributes (optional), and operations (optional). See Figure C-1 and the example that follows it.

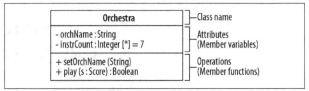

*Figure C-1. Class diagram*

```
// Corresponding code segment
class Orchestra { // Class Name
  // Attributes
  private String orch Name;
  private Integer instrCount = 7;
  // Operations
  public void setOrchName(String name) {...}
  public Boolean play(Score s) {...}
}
```

## Name

The name compartment is required and includes the class or interface name typed in boldface.

## Attributes

The attributes compartment is optional and includes member variables that represent the state of the object. The complete UML usage is as follows:

```
visibility name : type [multiplicity] = default
Value
{property-string}
```

Typically, only the attribute names and types are represented.

## Operations

The operations compartment is optional and includes member functions that represent the system's behavior. The complete UML usage for operations is as follows:

```
visibility name (parameter-list) :
return-type-expression
{property-string}
```

Typically, only the operation names and parameter lists are represented.

---

**TIP**

`{property-string}` can be any of several properties such as `{ordered}` or `{read-only}`.

---

## Visibility

Visibility indicators (prefix symbols) can be optionally defined for access modifiers. The indicators can be applied to the member variables and member functions of a class diagram (see Table C-1).

*Table C-1. Visibility indicators*

| Visibility indicators | Access modifiers |
|---|---|
| ~ | *package-private* |
| # | protected |
| - | private |

## Object Diagrams

Object diagrams are differentiated from class diagrams by underlining the text in the object's name compartment. The text can be represented in three different ways (see Table C-2).

*Table C-2. Object names*

| | |
|---|---|
| : ClassName | Class name only |
| objectName | Object name only |
| objectName : ClassName | Object and class name |

Object diagrams are not frequently used, but they can be helpful when detailing information, as shown in Figure C-2.

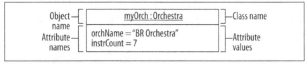

*Figure C-2. Object diagram*

# Graphical Icon Representation

Graphical icons are the main building blocks in UML diagrams (see Figure C-3).

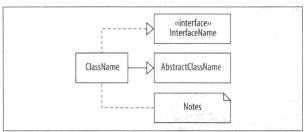

*Figure C-3. Graphical icon representation*

## Classes, Abstract Classes, and Interfaces

Classes, abstract classes, and interfaces are all represented with their names in boldface within a rectangle. Abstract classes are also italicized. Interfaces are prefaced with the word *interface* enclosed in guillemet characters. Guillemets house stereotypes and in the interface case, a classifier.

## Notes

Notes are comments in a rectangle with a folded corner. They can be represented alone, or they can be connected to another icon by a dashed line.

## Packages

A package is represented with an icon that resembles a file folder. The package name is inside the larger compartment unless the larger compartment is occupied by other graphical elements (i.e., class icons). In the latter case, the package name would be in the smaller compartment. An open arrowhead with a dashed line shows package dependencies.

The arrow always points in the direction of the package that is required to satisfy the dependency. Package diagrams are shown in Figure C-4.

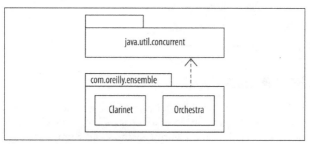

*Figure C-4. Package diagrams*

## Connectors

Connectors are the graphical images that show associations between classes. Connectors are detailed in "Class Relationships" on page 250.

## Multiplicity Indicators

Multiplicity indicators represent how many objects are participating in an association (see Table C-3). These indicators are typically included next to a connector and can also be used as part of a member variable in the attributes compartment.

*Table C-3. Multiplicity indicators*

| Indicator | Definition |
|-----------|------------|
| * | Zero or more objects |
| 0..* | Zero or more objects |
| 0..1 | Optional (zero or one object) |
| 0..n | Zero to $n$ objects where $n > 1$ |
| 1 | Exactly one object |
| 1..* | One or more objects |
| 1..n | One to $n$ objects where $n > 1$ |
| m..n | Specified range of objects |
| n | Only $n$ objects where $n > 1$ |

# Role Names

Role names are utilized when the relationships between classes need to be further clarified. Role names are often seen with multiplicity indicators. Figure C-5 shows Orchestra where it *performs* one or more Scores.

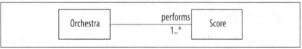

*Figure C-5. Role names*

# Class Relationships

Class relationships are represented by the use of connectors and class diagrams (see Figure C-6). Graphical icons, multiplicity indicators, and role names may also be used in depicting relationships.

## Association

An association denotes a relationship between classes and can be bidirectionally implied. Class attributes and multiplicities can be included at the target end(s).

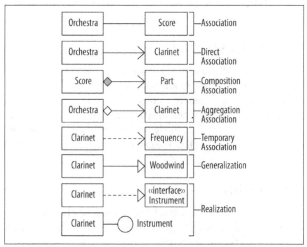

*Figure C-6. Class relationships*

## Direct Association

Direct association, also known as *navigability*, is a relationship directing the source class to the target class. This relationship can be read as "Orchestra has a Clarinet." Class attributes and multiplicities can be included at the target end. Navigability can be bidirectional between classes.

## Composition Association

Composition association, also known as *containment*, models a whole-part relationship, where the whole governs the lifetime of the parts. The parts cannot exist except as components of the whole. This is a stronger form of association than aggregation. This can be read as "Score is composed of" one or more parts.

## Aggregation Association

Aggregation association models a whole-part relationship, where the parts may exist independently of the whole. The whole does not govern the existence of the parts. This can be read as "Orchestra is the whole and Clarinet is part of Orchestra."

## Temporary Association

Temporary association, better known as *dependency*, is represented where one class requires the existence of another class. It's also seen in cases where an object is used as a local variable, return value, or a member function argument. Passing a frequency to a tune method of class Clarinet can be read as class Clarinet depends on class Frequency, or "Clarinet uses a Frequency."

## Generalization

Generalization is where a specialized class inherits elements of a more general class. In Java, we know this as inheritance, such as class extends class Woodwind, or "Clarinet is a Woodwind."

## Realization

Realization models a class implementing an interface, such as class Clarinet implements interface Instrument.

# Sequence Diagrams

UML sequence diagrams are used to show dynamic interaction between objects (see Figure C-7). The collaboration starts at the top of the diagram and works its way toward the bottom.

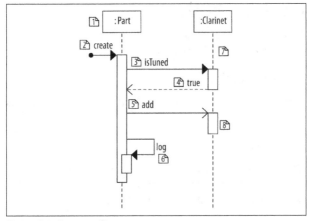

*Figure C-7. Sequence diagrams*

## Participant (1)

The participants are considered objects.

## Found Message (2)

A found message is one in which the caller is not represented in the diagram. This means that the sender is not known, or does not need to be shown in the given diagram.

## Synchronous Message (3)

A synchronous message is used when the source waits until the target has finished processing the message.

## Return Call (4)

The return call can optionally depict the return value and is typically excluded from sequence diagrams.

## Asynchronous Message (5)

An asynchronous message is used when the source does not wait for the target to finish processing the message.

## Message to Self (6)

A message to self, or *self-call*, is defined by a message that stays within the object.

## Lifeline (7)

Lifelines are associated with each object and are oriented vertically. They are related to time and are read downward, with the earliest event at the top of the page.

## Activation Bar (8)

The activation bar is represented on the lifeline or another activation bar. The bar shows when the participant (object) is active in the collaboration.

# Index

---

## About the Authors

**Robert James Liguori** is an Oracle Certified Java Professional and developer of several Java-based and Python-based aerospace and natural sciences applications.

**Patricia Liguori** is a multidisciplinary information systems engineer for The MITRE Corporation (*http://www.mitre.org/*) in the air traffic management domain.

## Colophon

The animal on the cover of *Java Pocket Guide* is the Javan tiger (*Panthera tigris sondaica*). In recent history, this extinct species lived on the island of Java in Indonesia, though fossil records indicate that as recently as 12,000 years ago, they also lived on Borneo Island and the Palawan archipelago.

Distinct for their long snouts, small frames, and relatively strong, powerful paws, these tigers subsisted on boars, deer, and wild cattle. Dutch writer J.G. ten Bokkel noted in 1890 that the locals would use an honorific title when referring to the animals ("Mister Tiger) for fear that discussing the animal in a familiar way would draw its ire.

Though efforts were made to conserve territory for these tigers as the population of Java expanded, a combination of hunting, industrial development, and civil unrest in the region drove the Javan tiger to extinction by 1994.

Many of the animals on O'Reilly covers are endangered. To learn more about how you can help, go to *animals.oreilly.com*.

The cover image is from the Dover Pictoral Archive. The cover fonts are URW Typewriter and Guardian Sans. The text font is Adobe Minion Pro; the heading font is Adobe Myriad Condensed; and the code font is Dalton Maag's Ubuntu Mono.

# Learn from experts.
# Find the answers you need.

Sign up for a **10-day free trial** to get **unlimited access** to all of the content on Safari, including Learning Paths, interactive tutorials, and curated playlists that draw from thousands of ebooks and training videos on a wide range of topics, including data, design, DevOps, management, business—and much more.

## Start your free trial at:
## oreilly.com/safari

(No credit card required.)

CPSIA information can be obtained
at www.ICGtesting.com
Printed in the USA
BVHW040905210521
607863BV00012B/170

9 781491 938690